Zero Waste Patterns

20 Projects to Sew Your Own Wardrobe

BIRGITTA
HELMERSSON

Photography by Emli Bendixen

quadrille

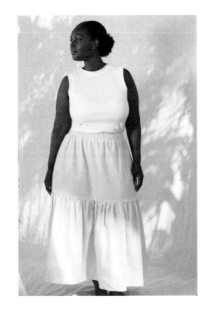

Introduction

At the age of 12, I started trying to make my own clothes. After my mum had seen me attempting to hand sew fabrics together for several months, she decided to buy me a sewing machine. With my clunky old second-hand Singer, I began taking apart my own clothes and trying to replicate the different shapes. I made some progress on my own, but it wasn't until five years later, after signing up to a local pattern-making class, that I really started to understand how much was possible. Once a week I would head out into the suburbs of my hometown of Perth, Western Australia, and sit in the back room of my teacher's home learning how to sew, the youngest in the room by at least three decades. In these first few classes I learnt step by step how to make a bodice, sleeve and skirt pattern block, fitted perfectly to my own measurements. I toiled them up in some rough calico and couldn't believe it when I tried them on: they fitted like a glove!

We went on to use these blocks as a foundation for everything we did, manipulating darts, adding in gathers and fullness, and combining the different blocks together. My teacher was very methodical in the way she taught, with decades of experience making made-to-measure garments. Learning from her made me feel as if the possibilities were endless and I will never forget how liberating those first few weeks felt! It had been my dream to study fashion design since I was 12, but after starting this first course I realized I wanted to learn in a much more hands-on way and explore the technical side of design in order to achieve my dream. I continued my education by working my way up through different jobs over the years, with the odd short course here and there, to gain the skills I was looking for.

Twenty years on from those first pattern-making classes, my method of pattern making has changed a lot. I work almost exclusively with zero waste pattern cutting now and I rarely use fitted pattern blocks any more. Although the pattern-making methods I work with are different to the ones I used in those early days, the overall concept I want to explore with this book is the same. I have carefully designed five zero waste blocks for you to use as your base pattern shapes, each one a classic wardrobe staple. Use each block as it is or explore a further 15 projects where you are guided through the steps of modifying the patterns into new designs.

For beginners and intermediate sewers alike, this will give you the confidence to begin making your own wardrobe using zero waste pattern cutting and should even serve as inspiration for you to draft your own designs from these shapes. I hope this book will give you that same feeling of excitement and joy that I experienced when my own pattern-making journey began all those years ago.

Why I work with zero waste pattern cutting (ZWPC)

ZWPC is a little like a puzzle. It is a method of pattern drafting where you utilize a pre-determined length of fabric end to end by strategically planning your pattern pieces so that every last scrap of fabric is used.

Before I became interested in ZWPC, I spent many years working as a pattern maker, seamstress and designer. I noticed there always seemed to be a way that was deemed 'correct', depending on which school you went to. Working in this way often felt quite rigid to me when all I wanted to do was cut straight from the fabric and play. Once I learnt the basics of pattern making, I very quickly went back to continuing my own self-exploration. I found it freeing being able to just drape things on my body or a mannequin and explore different shapes, without worrying too much about making mistakes.

After moving to Melbourne in my early twenties, I had the opportunity to work in many varied and creative jobs. I was very lucky to be able to work for small independent businesses that, for the time, were very sustainably and ethically minded, with local production and a lot of control over the fabrics and processes being used. But this was in the early 2000s and the conversation had really only just begun. Being in this very hands-on environment I was able to get a much fuller picture of how everything worked first hand, from design and development to visiting the factories and seeing the production process.

It was during this time that I started to become acutely aware of the textile waste that was being generated. I started to notice that the designs were always drawn first, often without much consideration of the fabric width being used, and then it was handed over to a pattern-maker to develop. Many of the designs were fairly efficient to cut, but there were many that were extremely wasteful.

As I started to notice the waste, I became more and more interested in exploring ways of reducing it, which led me to start looking into ZWPC. I instantly noticed that one

of the biggest differences in the ZWPC development process, compared to more conventional pattern-making methods, is that the design and pattern need to be worked on simultaneously. It is not just a matter of sitting down and drawing a design and then handing it off to a pattern maker to develop for you: instead, you always need to be thinking about how to strategically cut your designs so that they use everything, while being flattering on the body, efficient to cut and sew, and work across a range of sizes.

This new interest in ZWPC and my background in pattern making and sewing set me on a new path of exploration, which eventually culminated in founding my self-titled label in 2013, where I began experimenting more consistently with ZWPC. Right from the beginning I included zero waste designs in each collection, although usually just one or two styles. I opened a studio / store in Melbourne, where with a small team we did all of our production in house, and over the years I slowly began to add more zero waste designs to my 'pattern library'.

It wasn't until after my family and I had relocated to Sweden several years later that I finally made the decision to focus exclusively on ZWPC. My very first completely zero waste garment collection was supposed to be released online in 2020, literally days after the pandemic hit, and needless to say things got a little weird. I had already been sharing some images of the designs I had been working on in the lead-up to this. While we were sitting around figuring out how to move forward with everything, out of the blue we had some requests to make a sewing pattern. I thought it was such a great idea, although initially I saw it as a temporary offering. After the very first sewing pattern came out, the #zwcroppedshirt, I couldn't believe how quickly it took off. I realized that in order to really make a bigger impact with zero waste pattern cutting, I needed to actually give people the opportunity see how these garments were made.

The release of this first sewing pattern has inspired me to impart the knowledge and methods that I have developed in my own business over the years so that it can be more accessible. Learning to sew is so important. It teaches you the skills to make the clothes **you** want to wear, that **you** feel good in. It teaches you the skills to mend and care for your own clothes, treating them with love and appreciating them so that they last longer. And perhaps even more importantly, it opens your eyes to the time and resources that go into the making of a garment, so that you can have a deeper understanding of why it is so important to push for more ethical and sustainable practices in the fashion industry. With ZWPC I want you to take it one step further: by learning this method you will be more conscious of the waste being created while working on your own projects, which in turn will make you a far more conscious consumer overall.

What is a pattern block?

My concept with this book is to take the element of 'pattern blocks' used commonly in conventional pattern-making methods and incorporate this into zero waste pattern drafting and sewing.

A 'block' is a base pattern that is developed to be used by a pattern maker to draft patterns. These blocks can include, for example, a very basic version of a bodice, sleeve and skirt, which can be used on their own or combined to draft new designs such as a long-sleeved top or dress. Blocks can also include more developed patterns, such as a shirt with a collar or basic trousers. In my own experience of working with blocks, I have developed shapes that have been tried and tested over many years, which I know fit well and have flattering proportions. I use these blocks over and over every time I design a new garment or collection by making fit and design changes to them.

Pattern making is a highly skilled craft that can take many years to learn, which can be incredibly daunting for hobby sewists. By developing these zero waste blocks in classic wearable shapes, I have eliminated the technical and time-consuming work that goes into making your foundation pattern blocks, which means that you can now use these as they are to make your own wardrobe using zero waste pattern cutting.

How to use this book

This book is designed to be a workbook of classic shapes, all made using ZWPC. It consists of five blocks that can be used as stand-alone projects or modified to complete a further 15 projects. To make these garments you will not require any large paper patterns. All the designs are cut out by drawing the pattern pieces directly onto the fabric, with the help of small templates that you will find on the inside cover.

Blocks

The blocks are intended to show the concept of ZWPC, with each pattern fitting into a specific width and length of fabric, depending on your chosen size. Some of these blocks may not work for all fabric widths, but once you get to the projects, you will see how the blocks can be modified and used for specific fabric widths and made to fit entirely end to end.

All block samples have been made using organic cotton twill, 210 gsm, 165 cm (65 in.) wide, and some have the fabric cut to size in order to show the blocks made in different fabric widths and garment sizes. Any offcuts have been re-purposed into other garments, found in the projects section. All the blocks have detailed cutting plans, which can differ depending on your chosen size and fabric width, as well as detailed measurements by size, step-by-step cutting instructions and step-by-step sewing instructions with illustrations. For any instructions that are a bit more complex, refer to the Tools and Techniques chapter for more detailed information. The five blocks are:

- **Tee**: one size, size determined by fabric width
- **Trouser**: sizes XS–6XL
- **Singlet**: sizes XS–6XL
- **Skirt**: sizes XS–6XL
- **Shirt**: one size, size determined by fabric width

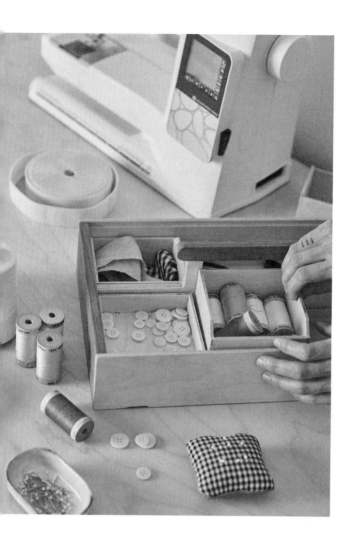

Skill level

Each block and project is given a skill level. Levels 1–2 are suitable for complete beginners, level 3 for confident beginners and levels 4–5 for intermediate to experienced sewers. If you are a true beginner and have not sewn before, start with a block or project that is at level 1 or 2 and work your way up.

Choose your size

Each block will clearly show pattern layouts with sizing information. Two standard sizings are used throughout.

SIZES XS–6XL

The Singlet, Trouser and Skirt blocks all have ten sizes, with different templates to be traced for each one. This size range is for a 90–150-cm (35½–59-in.) hip.

ONE SIZE

The Tee and Shirt blocks are one-size patterns where the sizing is largely determined by the fabric width you are using. These styles are oversized and include detailed charts on the maximum bust measurement possible when using different fabric widths. There is also an alternative cutting plan at the end of each of these blocks to show how you can size up the garment further.

Fabric widths

The recommended fabric widths vary depending on which pattern you are using, so refer to each block or project for more detailed information. Some of the blocks only work for very specific fabric widths, as these are used to show the concept of ZWPC. The projects are all made to be completely zero waste based on the fabric and size being cut out and show you how you can modify each pattern to your needs so that it fits end to end on your fabric.

When using narrower or wider widths, spend some time working out how you can change the position of your pattern pieces to make them fit end to end. If you do decide to cut off some areas so that your garment fits the way you want it to, then these offcuts will be rectangular or square in shape and therefore much easier to re-purpose into other projects.

In some projects, the length of the garment is determined by the fabric width you have chosen. All the garments are fairly loose-fitting, which gives you a huge degree of flexibility, so if you find a fabric that you really love the chances are that it will work with the cutting plan – and if it doesn't, it may be possible to insert a strip of another fabric to give you the width you need; see page 88.

Projects

The projects are simple modifications of the five blocks to make new designs. Each project includes information on which blocks and templates are used and what modifications need to be made to them, as well as the specific fabric width and length used. They are made in a specific garment size, with further tips and instructions on how to size up or down to fit your own measurements. To complete each project, always refer back to the block(s) used to find the main cutting and sewing instructions in your sizes.

Fabric types

The fabric you choose can have a huge impact on how well your garment turns out, so spend time selecting something that falls nicely and feels natural and beautiful to wear. If you are a beginner, then start by using stable fabrics such as woven cottons or structured linens. They will be much easier to cut and sew and will truly make your introduction to sewing a far smoother and more pleasurable experience.

WOVEN FABRICS

The majority of the projects in this book use woven fabrics, which do not have any stretch in them. The fabrics I love to use the most are linens and organic cottons, as well as re-purposed vintage and second-hand textiles. Start by searching your local charity shop or thrift store for textiles to see what you can find! I find that woven fabrics, in natural fibres such as cotton and linen, are easier to sew than knits and last a lot longer with wash and wear. They are often more sturdy and keep their shape longer.

STRETCH FABRICS

With this said however you can absolutely use knit fabrics as well if you find something you love – I just recommend that you choose something that is fairly structured, not too thin, of good quality, and that does not have too much stretch in it, to ensure that it is easier to work with and has a longer life.

PRINTS AND FABRICS WITH A NAP

Due to the zero waste nature of these patterns, pattern pieces usually need to be placed in a particular direction on the fabric so there may be some limitations when using one-directional prints or fabrics with a nap such as coating or corduroy. Keep this in mind when choosing a fabric for each project and check your pattern layout to see which direction your pieces lay across the fabric.

Tools and Techniques

Tools and notions

These are my recommendations for a basic tool kit to help you cut and sew zero waste patterns with ease. As these patterns are drawn straight onto the fabric, there are a few extra things you will want to add to your regular sewing kit that can make your life **a lot** easier. My top three go-to tools when working with zero waste patterns are a long right-angled ruler, a sharp piece of chalk or dissolvable fabric marker pen to help with drawing clear lines, and a calculator, to help with working out how to draw on your pattern pieces when using different fabric widths, or with any fit or design changes you want to make.

Here is my complete go-to list to make your cutting and sewing experience a smooth one...

TOOLS

• Sewing machine

• Overlocker/serger (alternatively you can use a zig-zag stitch, binding or a French seam to finish seam allowances – see page 14)

• Iron

• Long ruler, straight and/or right angle (this makes it easier to draw clear, straight lines directly onto the fabric)

• Tape measure

• Scissors: long dressmaking shears for cutting fabric and small scissors for trimming thread

• Pins

• Safety pin, for threading elastic through a casing

• Sharp tailor's chalk and/or dissolvable fabric marker pen for drawing clear, straight lines directly onto fabric

• Hand sewing needles

• Seam ripper for cutting open buttonholes

• Awl for marking darts

• Pencil, tape and paper for tracing templates

• Calculator

NOTIONS

These are some of the notions that you may need. Refer to the individual blocks and projects for more detailed measurements and instructions.

• Threads (for sewing machine and overlocker)

• Elastic (1 cm, 3 cm, 5 cm/ ⅜ in., 1¼ in., 2 in.)

• Cotton tape, 8 mm (⁵⁄₁₆ in.) wide

• Bias binding, 4 cm (1½ in.) wide

• Buttons in various diameters

Preparing and marking your fabric

Many fabrics will shrink a little when you first wash them and this is certainly true for most cottons and linens, which are used throughout this book. To account for shrinkage, buy around 5–10% more fabric than you need and pre-wash your fabrics before cutting and sewing. Make sure that you overlock (serge) or zig-zag any raw edges before washing to avoid too much fraying. You will need to iron and steam the piece after washing so that it is not too creased.

Before you can cut out the pattern pieces, you will need to cut the total fabric length (meterage/yardage) required and make sure that the cut edges have been straightened as much as possible. The total fabric length required is shown in each block and project description and may change depending on which fabric width/garment size you are using.

In most cases, the fabric is folded in half before being cut out. This is the preferred cutting method wherever possible as it means that the pieces will be cut much more neatly and evenly, particularly when cutting pairs (for example, a left and a right body, or a left and a right trouser leg). If the cutting plan requires you to cut on the fold, make sure you fold the fabric with the right sides of the fabric together, and fold in the correct direction.

There are two ways to fold: selvedge to selvedge (folding widthways) and cut edge to cut edge (folding lengthways). The cutting plans show which direction you need to fold.

MARKING OUT PATTERN PIECES

The easiest way to mark out pattern pieces is to use a sharp piece of tailor's chalk or a dissolvable fabric marker pen, and a metal ruler to ensure your lines are straight. As the pattern pieces are drawn directly onto the fabric, you need to make sure your cutting lines are easy to see and follow.

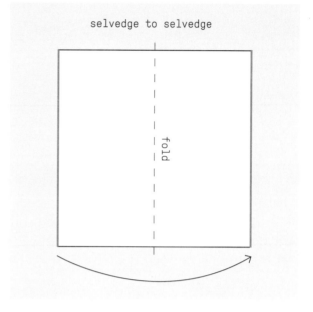

selvedge to selvedge

fold

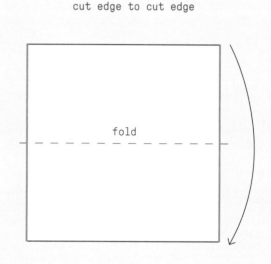

cut edge to cut edge

fold

Cutting

Each block and project has step-by-step cutting diagrams that show how to mark out and cut the pattern pieces. Different colours of line are used for different purposes (1) and below:

- **Blue line** indicates grainline/selvedge edge; the grainline runs along the same edge as the selvedge. The grainline edges are always marked with a blue line to show you how to orientate the pieces on the fabric.
- **Black line** indicates outline of pattern pieces.
- **Red line** indicates cut lines; where a red line is shown along a fold line, you need to cut apart these pieces exactly along the fold line.
- **Dashed line** indicates a fold line, the centre front or centre back, or the specific placement of measurements for pattern pieces.
- **Notch** indicates where to cut a notch to indicate how different pattern pieces join together or to show where to put for example darts and pocket bag openings. Notches should not be cut more than 5 mm (¼ in.) deep.

Here is an example on the right (2) of a cutting plan, showing the different lines used (the numbers indicate the order to follow when cutting the pieces apart):

TEMPLATES

All templates are on the inside cover of this book. Each block and project will clearly show which template(s), if any, are required. To use the templates, take a piece of paper and trace the templates you need to use, in the correct size. Different lines are used for different sizes (3). In some cases the templates may not fit onto one piece of paper, so you may need to join templates together. Always mark your traced template with the size and indicate what is the top and bottom to avoid confusion.

Making fit and design changes to the blocks - toiling and sampling

Every body is unique and therefore there may be some fit and design changes you want to make to each pattern so it fits you just the way you like it. As you work with each block, take a note of any changes you make to it, so that you have this information saved for next time.

Many people like to make a toile (a test garment in a cheap fabric such as calico to check the fit) before making the final garment in the 'good' fabric. This does, of course, take away from the zero waste aspect of these

1

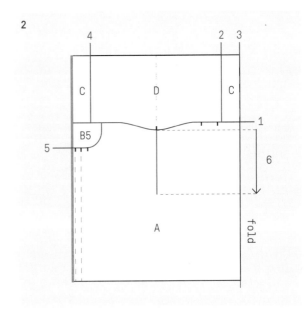

Grainline/selvedge edge

Outline of pattern pieces

Cut lines

Fold lines

Notch

2

3

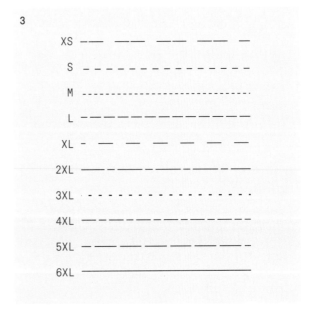

patterns. However, it's just as important to have a finished garment that you actually want to wear, that fits well and that you feel good in – otherwise there isn't much point in using a zero waste pattern in the first place, right? To solve this problem I recommend finding a balance between fit and waste by working with each of the blocks you like and making them up in a plain fabric, or by re-purposing some old unused textiles such as plain bed sheets. Once you have worked out which size suits you best, and any changes to fits and lengths you want to make, you can use these toiles as your 'master' samples.

Sewing techniques

All of the blocks have step-by-step sewing instructions with illustrations, but for any steps that require a little more explanation you can refer to these sewing techniques for further colour images and instructions. In some cases these techniques are specific to the zero waste aspect of these patterns, which means they may be a little different from more conventional sewing methods that you may have used before. They also include some neat little tips and tricks that I have learnt over the years to add finishes to your garments.

FINISHING SEAMS

All the seam allowances in this book are 1 cm (⅜ in.) unless otherwise specified.

Most of the seams in this book are finished with a line of straight stitching and overlocking (serging). We've specified overlocking throughout the instructions, but if you do not have an overlocker (serger), you can use zig-zag stitching and in many cases a French seam, to finish the edges neatly.

1 **Straight stitch:** Used to sew together one piece of fabric to another.

2 **French seam:** This encloses the raw edges and is most suitable for lightweight fabrics.

3 **Straight stitch and overlocking the seam allowances together:** The seam is pressed to one side and the overlocking is used to finish the raw edges neatly. If you do not have an overlocker, you can use a zig-zag stitch instead.

4 **Overlocking:** This is used when you overlock an edge separately. Usually when you overlock the edges separately the seams are then sewn together with a straight stitch afterwards and the seams are pressed open. The overlocking is used so that the raw edges do not fray. If you do not have an overlocker you can use zig-zag stitching instead.

5 **Zig-zag stitching:** If you do not have an overlocker, this can be used as an alternative to finish raw edges so they do not fray.

6 **Understitching:** This is used to hold back seams and is sewn on the facing or lining pieces. The seam allowance should always be pressed towards the lining or facing side and the stitch line should be very close to the seam to hold the seam down neatly here. This stitch line should never be visible from the right side of the garment.

7 **Binding** can also be used to finish some seams; see page 17.

Binding

Many of the blocks and projects in this book use binding to finish the edges. You can either buy pre-cut binding or cut and prepare your own from either an extra length of fabric that matches your project or an offcut of fabric in a contrasting colour. I always recommend cutting extra binding and sewing all of the pieces together to make one long continuous length. Save any leftover binding for future projects. There may be some small pieces of waste when cutting binding; these will be small triangles that you can save for a future patchwork project!

CUTTING BINDING STRIPS AND JOINING THEM TOGETHER

STEP 1   Cut a rectangle of fabric. It should be at least 30 cm (12 in.) long, so that your strips are long enough.

STEP 2   With the rectangle of fabric lying flat on the table, right side up, take the bottom left corner and fold it across and up on the diagonal so that the left short straight edge lines up with the top long straight edge of the fabric.

STEP 3   Now take the bottom right corner and fold the fabric across and up on the diagonal so that the bottom long straight edge lines up with the centre of the fabric, lining up with the first folded piece.

STEP 4   Now fold the fabric up and over, along the diagonal folded edge on the bottom right diagonal side.

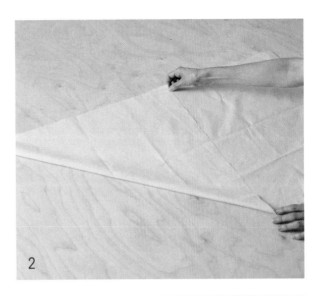

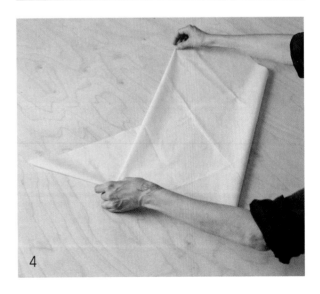

5

7

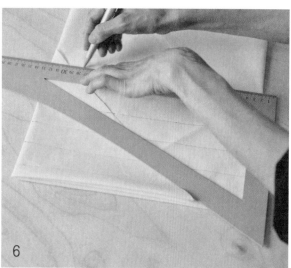

6

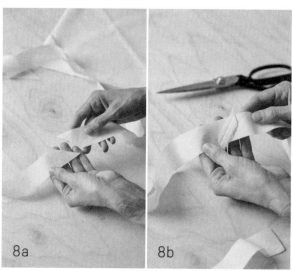

8a   8b

STEP 5   Finally, fold down the small remaining section on the top left so that the diagonal folded edges on the left are aligned.

STEP 6   Mark the first strip along the left side 2 cm (¾ in.) away from the folded edge, and then mark the remaining strips 4 cm (1½ in.) apart.

STEP 7   Cut the strips apart.

STEP 8   Place two strips at right angles to each other, right sides together, and stitch across, taking a 5-mm (¼-in.) seam allowance (8a). Press the seam open and trim off the little 'ears' that stick out (8b).

STEP 9   Loosely roll up the binding until required.

ATTACHING BINDING

These instructions use the Singlet block (page 56) as an example and also show how to make straps out of binding. Please note that if you are following these instructions to sew the singlet, make sure you attach the underarm tape first (see page 18) and then attach binding to the top front and back neck edges before attaching the underarm/strap binding.

STEP 1   Aligning the raw edges, with the right side of the binding against the wrong side of the garment, pin the binding in place (1a); you will need to very gently stretch it. Sew the binding to the wrong side of the garment, taking an 8-mm (⁵⁄₁₆-in.) seam allowance (1b). Where required, leave a strip of binding to be used as a strap (as in the Singlet block, page 56). The block or project sewing instructions will tell you how long a strip of binding you need.

STEP 2   Press the binding and seam allowances up and turn the garment over so that it's right side up.

STEP 3   Along the top raw edge of the binding, make two 1-cm (³⁄₈-in.) folds, so that the binding neatly covers the previous stitch line that is visible on the right side of the garment (3a). Press and pin in place (3b).

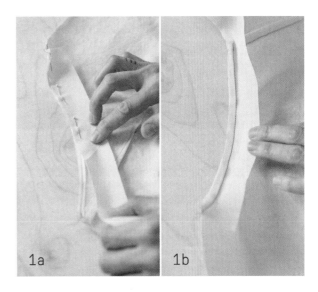

1a   1b

2

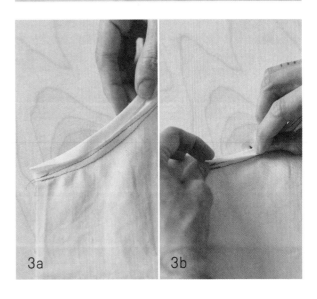

3a   3b

STEP 4   If you're using the binding to make straps, leave the required length of binding between the front and back bodices, then repeat steps 1 and 2 to apply binding to the wrong side of the back bodice. On the strap section, fold the top and bottom raw long edges of the binding in towards each other, 1 cm (⅜ in.), then fold through the centre of the binding all the way along. Your strap binding should look the same as the underarm binding and be even all the way along. Press and pin in place.

STEP 5   Working from the right side of the garment, topstitch the binding in place.

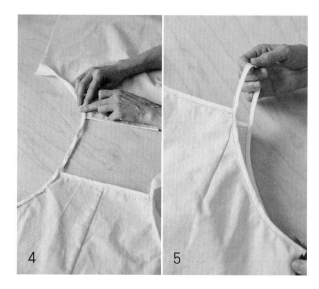

Underarm tape

Cotton tape is used to ease in the underarm on the Singlet block and several of the projects, so that the underarm doesn't gape when the garment is worn. It's important to add the tape before you attach the binding, otherwise the underarms can stretch out a lot. Cut the tape to length by following the instructions for your chosen project and size.

STEP 1   Pin the tape to the wrong side of the garment, aligning the long edge of the tape with the raw edge of the underarm all the way along. You will need to ease the tape onto the underarm so that it fits perfectly.

TIP   If you are having trouble easing your tape on (if the underarm seems too big, in other words), you can do a wide stitch along the underarm edge 5 mm (¼ in.) away from the raw edge, leaving a tail of thread on each end. Gently pull in the threads until the underarm is the same length as the tape and is evenly pulled in all the way along. This is similar to how you gather, but you just don't pull it in as much (see page 21).

STEP 2   Stitch the tape to the underarm, through the centre of the tape, making sure that the tape is right against the edge of the fabric.

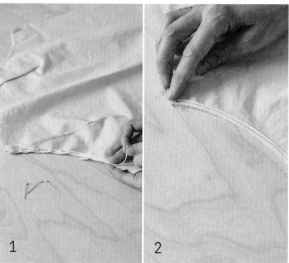

Inserting a sleeve

This technique shows how to insert the sleeve for the Shirt block and many of the projects using this pattern. The armhole on this pattern is a straight piece front and back, which means that the underarm point can be tricky to get right. Follow these steps to ensure you get a neatly sewn point at the underarm.

STEP 1   With your garment wrong side out and the sleeve right side out, pin the sleeve to the body, right sides of the fabric together. The sleeve notch on the centre shoulder should match the shoulder seam of the body and the sleeve underarm seam should match the very bottom of the armhole cut line.

STEP 2   Stitch the sleeve in place, making sure that you sew neatly into the underarm point. The stitch line should just cover the cut line, so that it is strong enough and there is no hole here, but also so that the underarm moves freely after sewing. Overlock (serge) the seam allowances together.

STEP 3   Press the armhole seam up into the body and check that the underarm looks neat from the right side of the garment without any hole here. Turn right side out.

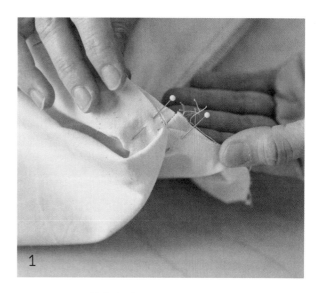

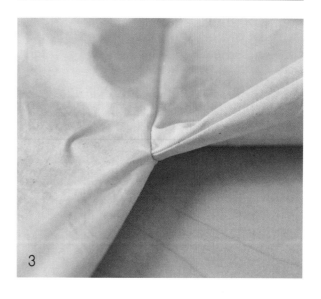

Elasticated waist casing

This technique is used in many of the projects in this book and is easier to do than applying a separate waistband. This same technique is used to make elasticated cuffs for the long-sleeved shirt.

STEP 1   Turn under and press the top edge of the waist to the wrong side of the garment all the way around (1a); the amount to press along this edge is specified for each block/project. Turn under and press the waist edge a second time (1b); again, the amount is specified for each block/project. Pin in place.

STEP 2   Stitch around the bottom of the waist casing from the inside of the garment, close to the fold, leaving an opening of about 5 cm (2 in.) at the centre back.

STEP 3   Attach a large safety pin to one end of the elastic and insert it into the waistband. Slide the elastic through all the way around.

STEP 4   Once the elastic is all the way through, ensure that it is not twisted and then overlap the ends by 1 cm (⅜ in.) and join them together with a zig-zag stitch or two rows of stitching.

STEP 5   Even out the elastic around the waistband so that it gathers in evenly and then stitch the opening at the back closed.

STEP 6   Finally, secure the elastic by stitching vertically through all layers at the centre front, centre back and both side seams. This ensures that the elastic will not twist with wash and wear.

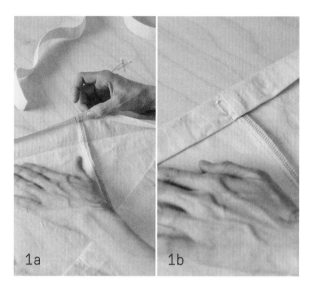

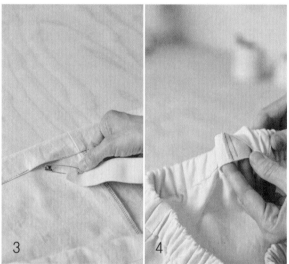

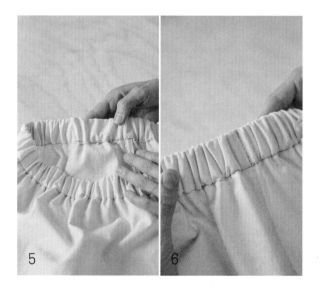

Gathers

I am definitely a lover of gathers, so of course this technique had to make it into the book! Gathers are used for the Skirt block and many of the projects. If you haven't sewn gathers before they can be tricky to get the hang of at first. Follow the steps below to get a beautiful neat gather every time.

STEP 1   Working inside the seam allowance, work two rows of stitching along the edge that needs to be gathered, starting 1 cm (⅜ in.) in from each side. Leave a tail of thread at both ends. If you are working with quite a long piece, such as a front and back panel already sewn together, work two rows of stitching separately on the front and back instead of working with the whole piece in one go (as you are more likely to have snapping threads when doing this, which is never fun!).

STEP 2   Gently pull the threads to gather the panel in to the desired width.

STEP 3   Gently pull the threads through from the front of the garment so that all four threads come through to the wrong side. Tie off both ends securely with three or four knots on each and trim away the excess threads.

STEP 4   Even out the gathers and check that the gathered panel is the same width as the panel to which it is to be attached.

STEP 5   With right sides together, pin the panel to the piece to which it is to be attached. Sewing with the gathered section uppermost, so that you can see that you are sewing the gathers neatly and evenly, stitch the panels together (5a). Overlock (serge) the seam allowances together and press the seam up (5b).

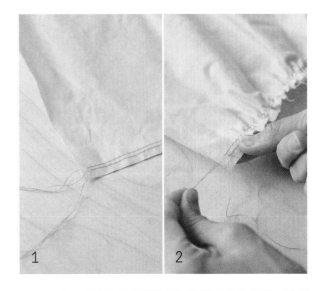

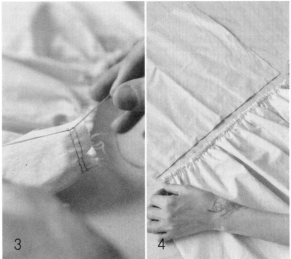

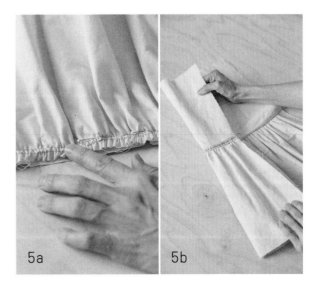

Patch pockets

Patch pockets are used for the Trouser block and any projects that use this pattern. The pockets for the Trouser block have a centre seam through them, as they are made using the pieces left over from cutting the front and back crotch. A patch pocket is also used for the Vintage shirt; the construction process is similar, but it does not have a centre seam and is not curved.

STEP 1   Place the two pocket pieces right sides together and sew the centre seam. Overlock (serge) the seam allowances together and press the seam to one side.

STEP 2   Press down the top of the pocket in line with the first notch (2a) and then again in line with the second notch (2b). Stitch from the wrong side, close to the fold.

STEP 3   Press the side and bottom edges to the wrong side by 1 cm (⅜ in.).

STEP 4   Pin the pocket to the garment, in the position specified in the project sewing instructions.

STEP 5   Topstitch the pocket in place and work a triangle of stitches at each top corner of the pocket to reinforce it.

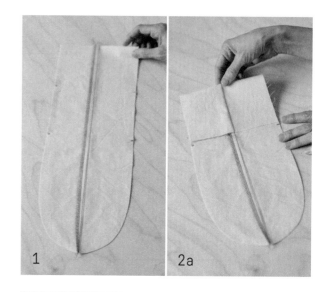

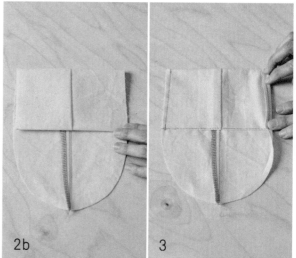

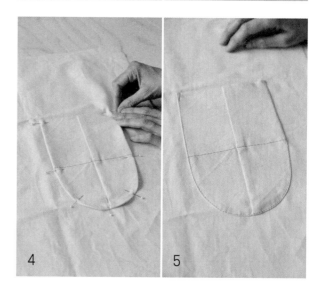

In-seam pockets

This is a method of sewing an in-seam pocket that I love using, because it makes a super-neat finish along the side seam – and once you learn the technique, it really is very easy to do. With this method the pocket bag is attached to the **front** of the garment only, before the front and back side seams are sewn together. It may be a little different from any method you have used before, so make sure you follow the steps carefully. This method is explained by using the pattern from the Triangle Skirt (page 158) as an example.

STEP 1   Place the two pocket bags together in pairs, right sides together. Sew along the un-notched side edge and the bottom edge, then overlock (serge) the seam allowances together.

STEP 2   With the front skirt right side up, line up one end of the pocket bag with the notch to the front side seam with the notch (2a). Now place this edge of the pocket bag on the front skirt, with right sides together (2b), and sew from the top down to the notch (2c). Snip into the notch further right up to the finished stitch point. Repeat with the other pocket bag on the other front side seam.

STEP 3   Press the pocket bag and seam allowances away from the front skirt and understitch close to the seam on the pocket bag side (3a), to hold the seam neatly down (3b).

2a

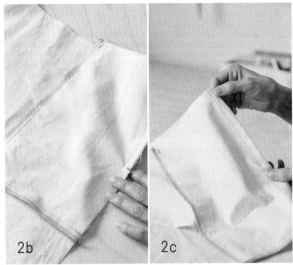

2b   2c

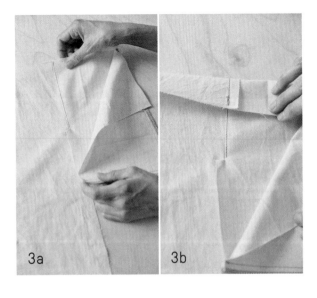

3a   3b

STEP 4 Turn the whole pocket bag to the wrong side of the garment, lining up the other straight edge of the pocket bag with the notch on front skirt side seam. This pocket bag edge becomes part of the front side seam at the top (4a and 4b). Topstitch the bottom part of your pocket bag in place on the front side seam, below the notch, to hold it down neatly. Make sure your stitch line goes right up the finished point of the snipped notch point; this will be approximately 1 cm (⅜ in.) away from the raw edge (4c).

STEP 5 Line up the front and back skirt side seams (5a). Place the front and back right sides together and sew the side seams (5b). The top part of the pocket bag should be treated as part of the front skirt side seam; make sure you keep the rest of the pocket bag out of the way as you sew and also that you just manage to cover the first stitch line that is holding the bottom part of the pocket bag down to the front side seam.

STEP 6 Overlock the seams together and press the seams towards the back (overlocking is not shown in the photos). Turn the garment right side out and check that your pocket opening is kept free and that it is neat at the notch point, which is the bottom part of the pocket opening.

STEP 7 Finally, you may need to secure the top part of your pocket bag across the top of the skirt (but this does depend on which project you are working with). Pin the top of the pocket bag neatly in place across the top raw edge of the front skirt and topstitch in place.

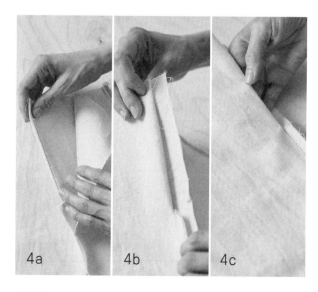

4a   4b   4c

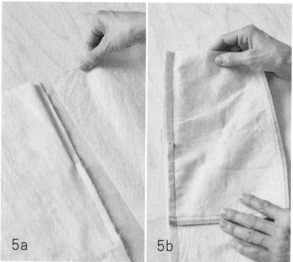

5a   5b

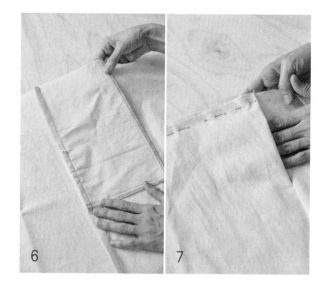

6   7

Sewing and attaching a collar and button placket

Attaching the collar to the Shirt block has a few extra steps to ensure that the neck sits nicely at the shoulder seam point. This technique is also used in several of the projects. Before starting these steps, make sure that you have already sewn the back pleat and shoulder seams. Also prepare the back neck facing by sewing the centre back seams together and attaching a binding to the curved edge. These steps are explained in more detail in the Shirt block (page 78). The shirt placket is created by folding the front in twice, instead of attaching a separate button placket. If you are using a very lightweight fabric, you can apply a lightweight iron-on interfacing before sewing. Apply to the wrong side of the centre front edges of the front bodies, up to the second notch, and fuse all the way along. Also apply interfacing to the wrong side of one of the collar pieces (i.e.: one pair sewn together at the centre back) before sewing.

STEP 1   With right sides together, pin the collar pieces together in two pairs and sew the centre back seams. Press the seams open.

STEP 2   Place the two pairs right sides together, making sure the centre back seams match, and sew along one long edge.

STEP 3   Open out the piece. Press the seam down and understitch along this edge, close to the seam, to hold the seam allowance down neatly. This side will be the underside of your collar.

STEP 4   Fold the collar in half, right sides together, and stitch across both short ends.

STEP 5   Turn the collar right side out (5a) and press (5b).

STEP 6   Sew along the long raw edges, stitching 5 mm (¼ in.) from the edge.

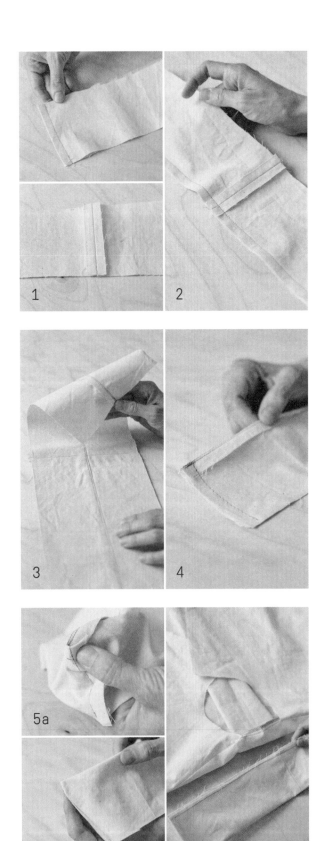

STEP 7   Pin the long collar edge sewn in step 5 to the shirt neck, with the underside of the collar (the side that has the understitching) against the right side of the shirt body (7a). Make sure that the centre back seam of the collar matches the centre back pleat. Line up each end of the collar with the correlating notches on the front shirt neck, the third notch away from the centre front edges. Stitch in place. When stitching the collar across the shoulder seam, make sure that the seam is sitting correctly; the shoulder seam should be pressed towards the back (7b).

STEP 8   Attach a length of binding to the front neck only, covering the seam that the collar is attached to. Start at the second notch away from the centre front edge of the shirt and continue up to the shoulder seam point only. Leave a loose tail of binding (around 5 cm/ 2 in.) past each shoulder point.

STEP 9   With right sides together, matching the centre back seams, place the centre back facing piece on the back neck on the collar side (9a). Pin the back facing down and stitch between the shoulder seams only (9b), making sure you keep the loose tails of binding free.

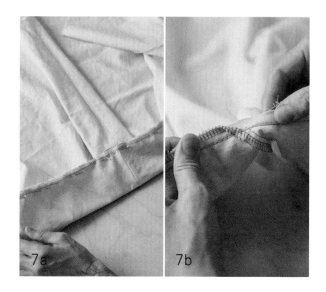

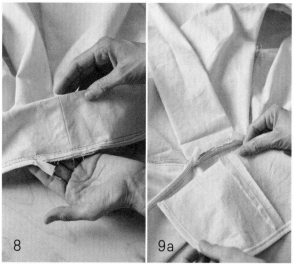

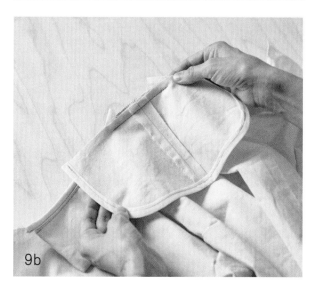

STEP 10   Press the facing and seam allowances away from the collar and body, then understitch along the facing side close to the seam to hold down the seam allowances neatly between the shoulder points.

STEP 11   Attach the remaining ends of the back neck facing to the left and right shoulder seams, right sides together; the loose ends of binding (11a) will need to be caught in at a right angle so that the back shoulder and neck sit flat and neat (11b and 11c). Press the seams towards the back.

STEP 12   Press down the facing and pin it to the wrong side of the back shirt so that it sits over the pleat (12a). Working from the wrong side, stitch the curved edge to the back body (12b), creating a decorative stitch feature that's visible on the right side of the garment (12c).

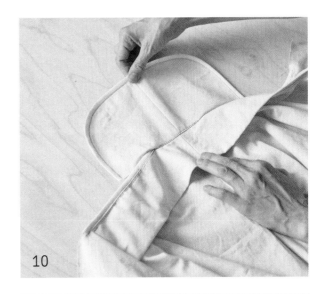

10

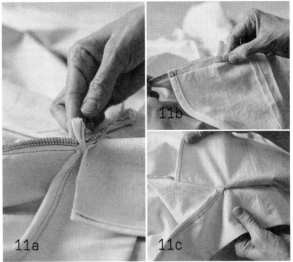

11a   11b   11c

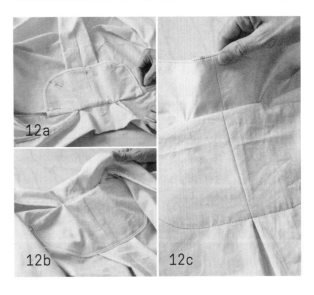

12a   12b   12c

STEP 13   Now stitch the button placket. With right sides together, turn back the centre front edges to the second notch (13a), then turn the centre front edges the other direction to the first notch, wrong sides together (13b). Pin together at the top along the folds and gently press the second fold in place. Topstitch in place along the top edge to hold these folds down, taking a 1-cm (⅜-in.) seam allowance (13c). The bound edge on the front neck should be covered by this seam.

STEP 14   Turn the placket the right way out (14a) and then press along the centre front edge so that the placket is the same width all the way down. Pin in place. Working from the inside of the garment, stitch all the way down the placket close to the fold (14b and 14c).

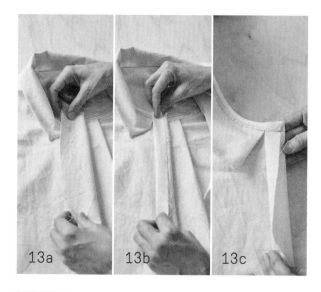

13a   13b   13c

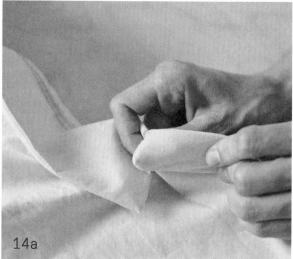

14a

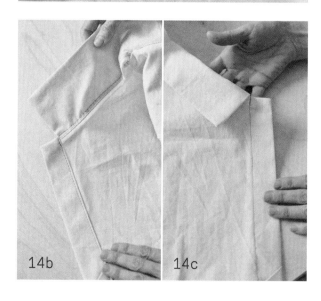

14b   14c

Buttons and buttonholes

Buttonholes and buttons are featured on the Shirt block and in several of the projects. Refer to your sewing machine manual for details of how to sew buttonholes. Refer to each block/project for details of where to position the buttonholes and whether they should be placed vertically or horizontally.

STEP 1   Mark your buttonholes on one side (placket) of your garment. The buttonholes should be the same width as the button you are using.

STEP 2   Sew the buttonholes using your machine. Open the buttonholes through the centre (2a), making sure that you don't accidentally cut through any of the stitching (2b). Use a seam ripper to make this cut, or a pair of small sharp scissors.

TIP   When using a seam ripper, put the sharp point into the start of your buttonhole, cut through a small amount, then push the sharp point out through the finished point of your buttonhole on the other side, and then cut open the remainder. A seam ripper is a great way to open buttonholes but it can also be very sharp, so doing it this way ensures that you don't accidentally cut through more fabric than you intend to!

STEP 3   Sew buttons to the other placket corresponding to the buttonholes.

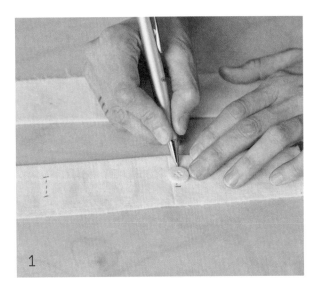

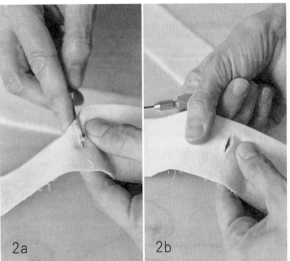

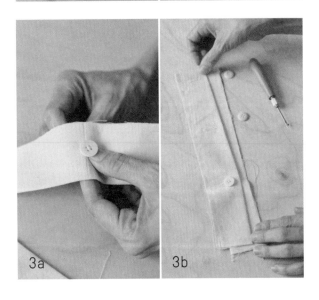

Blocks

This oversized boxy tee is a one-size garment in which the total body circumference is determined by the width of the fabric you are using.

Tee

It has a curved neck at the front and a V-neck at the back, as well as side splits that are faced using pieces cut out at the front and back necklines. The neckline is finished with bias binding. The pattern is simple and fun, with the shape formed by drawing equal-sized squares that slot together a bit like Tetris. Tips are included on how to size up the tee using an alternative pattern layout.

The sample is made using 135-cm (53-in.) wide organic cotton twill.

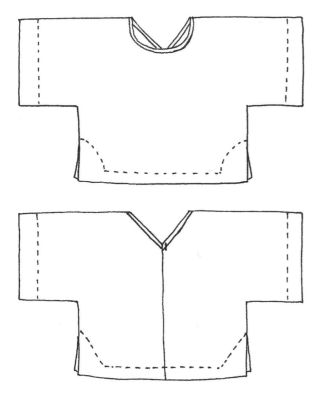

TECHNIQUE USED
Binding (page 15)

PROJECTS
This block is used in the Fold-back Collar Dress (page 92), Sweater (page 98), Wrap Top (page 104) and Boiler Suit (page 110).

SUITABLE FABRIC WIDTHS
The recommended widths are 125–165 cm (49–65 in.). Keep in mind that, as this is a one-size garment, the body circumference will get bigger or smaller depending on the fabric width you are using. Check the size chart to see which fabric widths will work for your measurements. If your measurements do not work for the width of fabric you want to use, then refer to Pattern adjustment tips for more information.

FABRIC TYPE
This style works really well in woven fabrics such as cotton or linen in a light-to-medium weight of 90–200 gsm.

NOTIONS
70 cm (27½ in.) bias binding, 4 cm (1½ in.) wide, to finish the neck.

TEMPLATE (SEE INSIDE COVER)
B1 Front split facing

B1

SIZE CHART

The size of this garment depends on the width of the fabric you use. This size chart accounts for around 25 cm (10 in.) ease from the actual garment measurements and shows the **maximum** chest/bust and hip measurement recommended for each fabric width. As the tee is meant to be oversized, you can still work with a wider fabric even if your measurements are a lot smaller than the maximum stated below – see Fabric adjustment tips: Sizing up, page 43. Ideally, however, your measurements should be no more than 25 cm (10 in.) smaller than the maximum shown below.

FABRIC WIDTH	MAX. CHEST/BUST	MAX. HIP
125 cm (49 in.)	94 cm (37 in.)	98 cm (38½ in.)
130 cm (51 in.)	99 cm (39 in.)	103 cm (40½ in.)
135 cm (53 in.)	104 cm (41 in.)	108 cm (42½ in.)
140 cm (55 in.)	109 cm (43 in.)	113 cm (44½ in.)
145 cm (57 in.)	114 cm (45 in.)	118 cm (46½ in.)
150 cm (59 in.)	119 cm (47 in.)	123 cm (48½ in.)
155 cm (61 in.)	124 cm (49 in.)	128 cm (50½ in.)
160 cm (63 in.)	129 cm (51 in.)	133 cm (52½ in.)
165 cm (65 in.)	134 cm (53 in.)	138 cm (54½ in.)

CUTTING PLAN

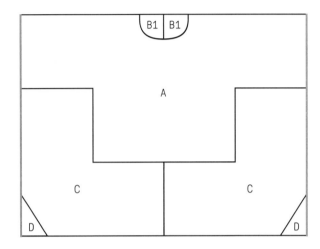

A Front body/sleeve

B Front split facing (template B1)

C Back body/sleeve

D Back split facing

Cutting

STEP 1   To calculate the length of fabric you need based on your fabric width, use the following formula:

(Fabric width ÷ 4) x 3 = length

So for a piece of fabric 140 cm (55 in.) wide, your length will be 105 cm (41¼ in.).

Cut your fabric to length and fold it in half widthways, with right sides together.

STEP 2   Prepare to mark out the pattern pieces by dividing the folded fabric into equal-sized squares. Start by dividing the fabric into two equal parts across the width and into three equal parts along the length, marking the points with chalk or a dissolvable fabric marker pen.

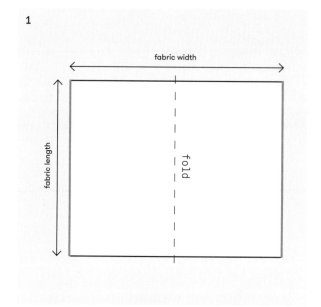

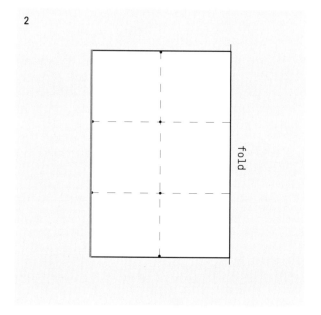

STEP 3   Draw in the front and back body/sleeve pieces with a ruler, and then place the front split facing template (B1) on the top right of the fabric, on the fold line of the front body and draw around it. Draw in the back split facing (D) by measuring 10 cm (4 in.) up and 10 cm (4 in.) across from the bottom left.

STEP 4   Cut the pieces apart in order from 1 to 5.

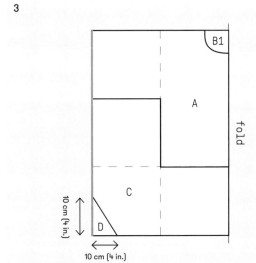

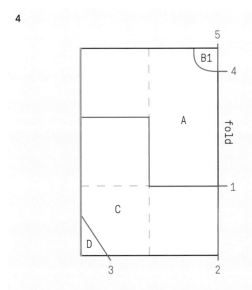

Sewing

1. Neck

STEP 1a   Place the front and back bodies (A and C) right sides together and sew the shoulder seams. Overlock (serge) the seam allowances together, then press the seams towards the back.

STEP 1b   Bind the neckline with the bias strip (see page 17), leaving a little bit of excess overhanging at each end.

STEP 1c   With right sides together, sew the centre back seam, then overlock the raw edges together. Make sure the sides of the V on the back line up neatly, then trim off any excess binding. Press the centre back seam to one side, then stitch over the binding through all layers to neaten and hold the seam in place.

1a

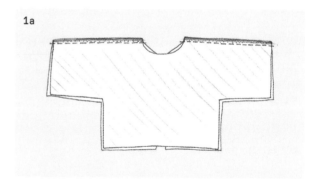

1b

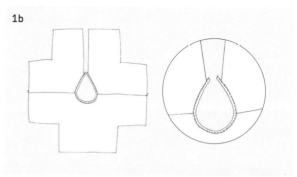

1c

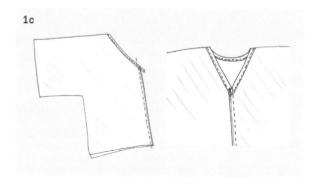

2. Side seams and splits

STEP 2a   Snip into all four underarm points on the front and back bodies (A and C). Overlock all four side seams separately from sleeve hem to body hem.

STEP 2b   Press under the curved edge of the front split facings (B1) to the wrong side by approximately 1 cm (⅜ in.). Press the angled bias edge of the back hem facings (D) to the wrong side by approximately 1 cm (⅜ in.).

STEP 2c   With right sides together, stitch the curved front split facings (B1) to the bottom edge of the front hems (A) and the triangular back split facings (D) to the bottom edge of the back hems (C). Press the facings down and then press the hem to the wrong side by 1 cm (⅜ in.) all the way around the front and back body pieces.

STEP 2d   Decide how long you want your tee to be and mark the finished hem length with a notch on all four side seams. Now measure from this notch to the top of the facings: this will give you your split length. Mark this length with a notch on all four side seams by measuring up from your finished hem length. The turn-up here can vary depending on the fabric width you have used, but as a guide an ideal finished length, measured from the shoulder, is 55–60 cm (21½–23½ in.).

2a

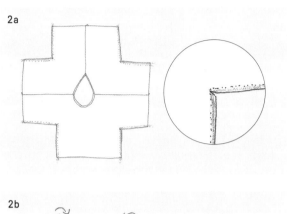

2b

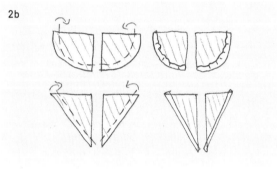

2c

2d

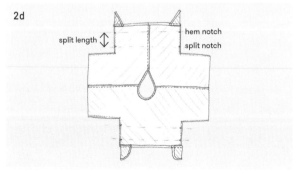

split length ↕   hem notch

split notch

STEP 2e   With right sides together, sew the side seams from the sleeve hem to the split notch that you marked in step 2d. Press the seams open.

STEP 2f   With the garment right side out, turn up the front along the finished hem line, so that the tops of the facings align with the split notches. Stitch from the top of the facing down to the hem. Turn the facings and hem to the wrong side of the garment. Make sure the hem is level all the way around, then press well. Repeat on the back of the garment.

STEP 2g   Press up the hems of the body all the way around and pin in place. Working from the wrong side, stitch all around the hem, making sure you follow the shape of the side split facings.

3. Sleeve hems

STEP 3   Press under the raw ends of the sleeves by 1 cm (3/8 in.), then press up the hems of the sleeves to your preferred length. Pin and topstitch in place.

2e

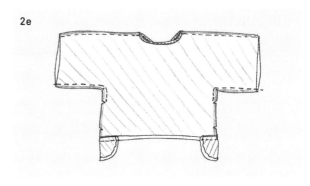

2f

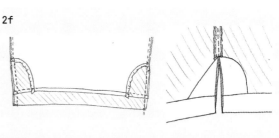

2g

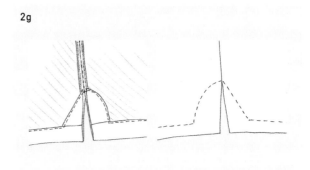

3

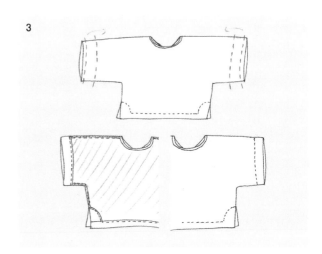

Fabric adjustment tips

SIZING UP

If your fabric width will not allow for a large enough garment for your own measurements, then you can adjust your cutting plan accordingly. This cutting plan is not recommended for fabric widths above 135 cm (53 in.), as it may become too oversized. Keep in mind that, as this block is based on equal-sized squares, as you size up the body and sleeves will also get longer.

STEP 1   To calculate the length of fabric you need based on your fabric width, use the following formula:

(Fabric width ÷ 3) x 4 = length

So for a piece of fabric 130 cm (51 in.) wide, your length will be 173 cm (68 in.).

STEP 2   Check the sizing.

Maximum bust measurement = total fabric length minus 30 cm (12 in.)

So for a piece of fabric 130 cm (51 in.) wide, your maximum bust measurement will be 143 cm (56 in.).

1

These high-waisted, full-length trousers have straight legs, an elasticated waist and back patch pockets.

Trouser

It's a really simple make and it's easy to adjust the lengths. You can also add shaping into the side seams with darts. The pattern has 10 sizes and each size works for a very specific fabric width. Tips are included on how to change the cutting plan for other fabric widths.

The sample is a size L, made using 150-cm (59-in.) wide organic cotton twill.

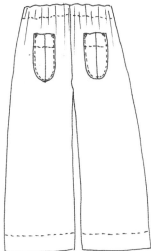

SKILL LEVEL ●●○○○

TECHNIQUES USED

Elasticated waist casing (page 20), Patch pockets (page 22)

PROJECTS

This block is used in the Boiler Suit (page 110), Shorts (page 120) and Playsuit (page 126).

SUITABLE FABRIC WIDTHS

The recommended widths for the trousers change depending on the size you are making. See cutting plan step 1 on page 50 for more information. For wider widths you can change the pattern layout to go in the other direction on the fabric, with the waist and hems running along the selvedge edges; refer to Pattern adjustment tips on page 55 for more information.

FABRIC TYPE

Woven fabrics in cotton or linen in a structured medium weight of 200–250gsm. This style would also work well in a softer fabric such as a heavy viscose or heavy silk, and also in light- or medium-weight wool suiting.

NOTIONS

Elastic, 5 cm (2 in.) wide, for the waist – see the elastic size chart below for cut lengths by size

Note: these are recommended lengths only and you may want to fit elastic to your own measurement.

XS	S	M	L	XL	2XL	3XL	4XL	5XL	6XL
60 cm	65 cm	70 cm	75 cm	80 cm	85 cm	91 cm	97 cm	103 cm	109 cm
23½ in.	25½ in.	27½ in.	29½ in.	31½ in.	33½ in.	35¾ in.	38 in.	40½ in.	43 in.

TEMPLATE (SEE INSIDE COVER)

B2 Back pocket

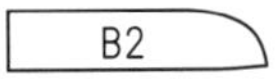

SIZE CHART

	WAIST RANGE	MAX. HIP	CROTCH LENGTH
XS	62–70 cm (24½–27½ in.)	90 cm (35½ in.)	78.5 cm (30¾ in.)
S	67–75 cm (26½–29½ in.)	95 cm (37½ in.)	80.5 cm (31½ in.)
M	72–80 cm (28½–31½ in.)	100 cm (39½ in.)	82.5 cm (32¼ in.)
L	77–85 cm (30½–33½ in.)	105 cm (41½ in.)	84.5 cm (33 in.)
XL	82–90 cm (32½–35½ in.)	110 cm (43½ in.)	86.5 cm (33¾ in.)
2XL	87–95 cm (34½–37½ in.)	118 cm (46½ in.)	88.5 cm (34¾ in.)
3XL	95–103 cm (37½–40½ in.)	126 cm (49½ in.)	90.5 cm (35½ in.)
4XL	103–111 cm (40½–43½ in.)	134 cm (52½ in.)	92.5 cm (36¼ in.)
5XL	111–119 cm (43½–46½ in.)	142 cm (56 in.)	94.5 cm (37 in.)
6XL	119–127 cm (46½–49½ in.)	150 cm (59 in.)	96.5 cm (37¾ in.)

CUTTING PLAN

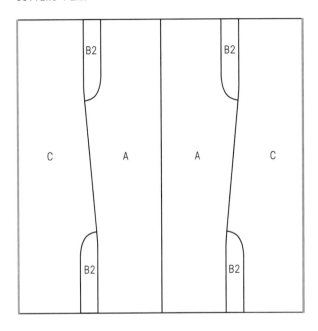

A   Front leg

B   Back pocket (template B2)

C   Back leg

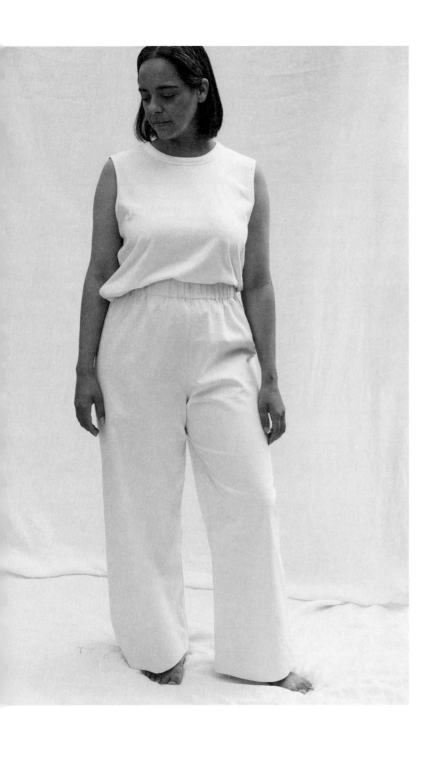

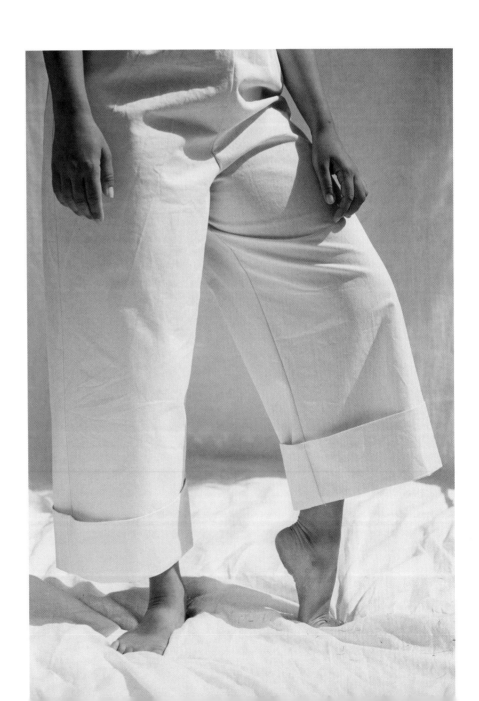

Cutting

STEP 1

	FABRIC WIDTH	FABRIC LENGTH
XS	135 cm (53 in.)	120 cm (47 in.)
S	140 cm (55 in.)	120 cm (47 in.)
M	145 cm (57 in.)	120 cm (47 in.)
L	150 cm (59 in.)	125 cm (49 in.)
XL	155 cm (61 in.)	125 cm (49 in.)
2XL	160 cm (63 in.)	125 cm (49 in.)
3XL	165 cm (65 in.)	130 cm (51 in.)
4XL	170 cm (67 in.)	130 cm (51 in.)
5XL	175 cm (69 in.)	130 cm (51 in.)
6XL	180 cm (71 in.)	130 cm (51 in.)

Note: For wider fabrics, place your pattern pieces going in the other direction on your fabric – see Pattern adjustment tips (page 55) for more information.

Referring to the chart above, cut your fabric to the length required for your size and fold it in half widthways, right sides together.

STEP 2

	WAIST/POCKET
XS	36.5 cm (14½ in.)
S	38 cm (15 in.)
M	39.5 cm (15¾ in.)
L	41 cm (16¼ in.)
XL	42.5 cm (16¾ in.)
2XL	44 cm (17½ in.)
3XL	46.5 cm (18¼ in.)
4XL	49 cm (19¼ in.)
5XL	51.5 cm (20¼ in.)
6XL	54 cm (21¼ in.)

1

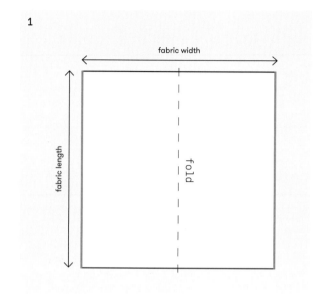

2

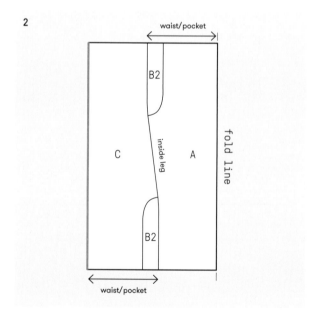

STEP 2 CONTINUED   Find the waist/pocket measurement for your size from the chart on page 50. Along the top edge of the fabric, measure this distance from the fold and make a mark. Line up the B2 template in the correct size with this mark and draw around the template. Repeat, this time measuring from the bottom left edge of the fabric. Mark one more straight line to join up the templates from bottom edge to bottom edge. This line becomes the inside leg.

STEP 3   Cut the pieces apart in order from 1 to 4.

STEP 4   Mark notches on the pockets (B2) using the template. Referring to the diagram, mark notches on the front and back trouser pieces. The notches are the same for all sizes. Please note that the side seam and centre front notches sit a little lower than the centre back notches; this allows for the centre back of the trousers to sit a little higher on your body.

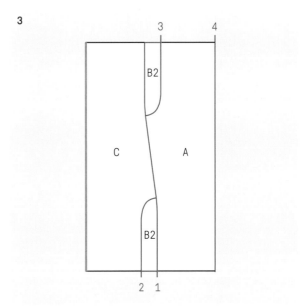

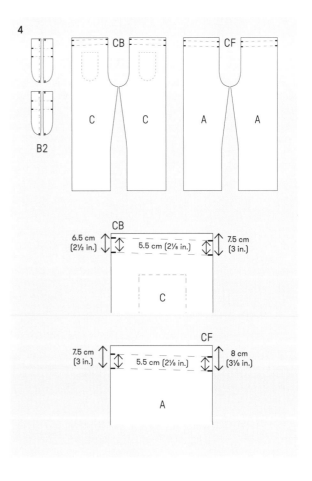

Sewing

1. Pockets

STEP 1a Prepare the back pockets, following steps 1–3 of Patch pockets on page 22.

STEP 1b Measure 18 cm (7 in.) down from the waist of each back trouser leg and pin the pockets in the centre. Topstitch the pockets to the legs, then sew a reinforcing triangle (see page 22) in the top corner of each pocket.

2. Side, crotch and inside leg seams

STEP 2a Place the front and back legs right sides together and sew the crotch seams. Overlock the seam allowances together. Press the seam allowances towards the left front on the front trouser and towards the right back on the back trouser, so that the seams will be offset when you sew the inside leg seams in step 2d.

STEP 2b With right sides together sew the side seams, then overlock the seam allowances together. Press the seam allowances towards the back.

STEP 2c
OPTIONAL These trousers have very straight side seams, so if you would like to add some shape from the waist to the hip, you can add in this optional shaping. The recommended amount to take in is 2–4 cm (¾–1½ in.). (The example right shows the sides taken in by 2.5 cm/1 in.) Start the shaping 5.5 cm (2⅛ in.) past the second waist casing notch and gently curve the line outwards for approximately 28 cm (11 in.); the rest of the seam allowance along the side seam should be the standard 1 cm (⅜ in.). This shaping will need to be done for both side seams.

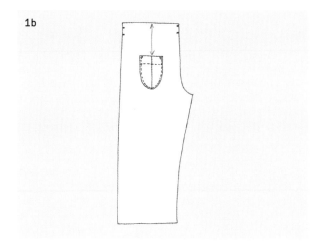

1b

2a

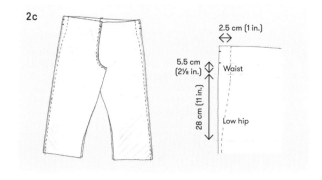

2c

2.5 cm (1 in.)

5.5 cm (2⅛ in.) Waist

28 cm (11 in.) Low hip

STEP 2d   With right sides together, sew the inside leg seams. Overlock the seam allowances together, making sure that you offset the front and back crotch seams to reduce bulk.

3. Waist casing

STEP 3a   Turn under and press the top edge of the waist as far as the first notch, then press down the waist to the second notch all the way around. (Keep in mind that the waist turns down more at the front than the back, as the back waist sits slightly higher.) The finished width of the waist casing should be 5.5 cm (2⅛ in.). Stitch around the bottom of the waist casing, leaving an opening of about 5 cm (2 in.) at the centre back to thread the elastic through.

STEP 3b   Insert and secure the elastic, following steps 2–5 of Elasticated waist casing on page 20.

4. Hem

STEP 4   To hem the legs, turn 1 cm (⅜ in.) to the wrong side and press, then try on the trousers and turn up the hem to your chosen length. Press and pin the hem in place, measuring to make sure you have turned up the same amount all the way around. Topstitch all around.

2d

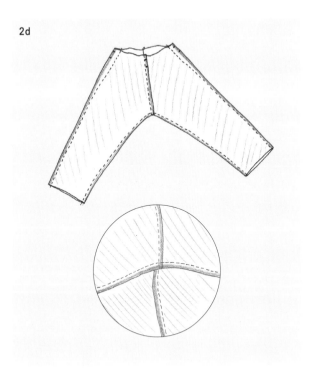

3a

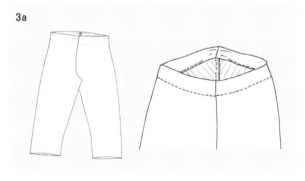

4

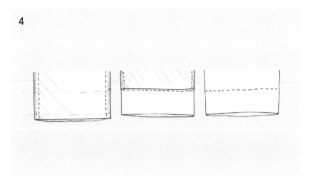

Pattern adjustment tips

USING DIFFERENT FABRIC WIDTHS

Place your pattern pieces going the other direction on your fabric, so that the hem and waist are in line with the selvedge and folded edge. Your width becomes your length and your length becomes your width. Using this layout means that your finished length is determined by your fabric width. The minimum recommended width is 115 cm (45 in.) and the maximum recommended width is 140 cm (55 in.).

A   Front leg

B   Back pocket (template B2)

C   Back leg

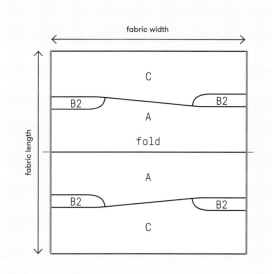

This singlet is a relaxed fit, with binding used to finish the neck and armholes as well as to make the straps.

Singlet

The armhole cut-outs are used to face the side-seam splits and there are small darts on the front body for bust shaping. The singlet has ten sizes and each size works for a very specific fabric width and length. Tips are included on how to change the layout for other fabric widths.

The sample is a size M, made using organic cotton twill.

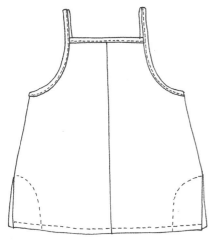

SKILL LEVEL ●●○○○

TECHNIQUES USED
Underarm tape (page 18), Binding (page 15)

PROJECTS
This block is used in the Playsuit (page 126), Sun Dress (page 134), Patchwork Singlet (page 140) and Slip Dress (page 146).

SUITABLE FABRIC WIDTHS
The recommended widths for the singlet change depending on the size you are making. See cutting plan step 1 on page 62 for more information. To use different widths of fabric, refer to Pattern adjustments tips on page 67 for more information.

FABRIC TYPE
This works really well in woven fabrics such as cotton or linen in a light-to-medium weight of 90–200 gsm. This style looks beautiful in laundered linen and even in a more structured cotton twill.

NOTIONS
Cotton tape, 8 mm (5/16 in.) wide. You will need four lengths for the front and back underarms. Size chart below:

XS	S	M	L	XL	2XL	3XL	4XL	5XL	6XL
22.5 cm	23.5 cm	24.5 cm	25.5 cm	26 cm	27 cm	27.5 cm	28.5 cm	29 cm	30 cm
8⅞ in.	9¼ in.	9⅝ in.	10 in.	10¼ in.	10⅝ in.	10⅞ in.	11¼ in.	11½ in.	11⅞ in.

Binding, 4 cm (1½ in.) wide. You will need two lengths to finish the front and back neck. Size chart below:

XS	S	M	L	XL	2XL	3XL	4XL	5XL	6XL
21 cm	22 cm	23 cm	24 cm	25 cm	26 cm	27 cm	28 cm	29 cm	30 cm
8¼ in.	8½ in.	9 in.	9½ in.	10 in.	10¼ in.	10½ in.	11 in.	11½ in.	12 in.

Binding, 4 cm (1½ in.) wide. You will need two lengths to finish the front and back armholes/straps. Size chart below:

XS	S	M	L	XL	2XL	3XL	4XL	5XL	6XL
58 cm	62 cm	65 cm	69 cm	72 cm	76 cm	79 cm	83 cm	86 cm	90 cm
23 in.	24½ in.	25½ in.	27 in.	28½ in.	30 in.	31 in.	32¾ in.	34 in.	35½ in.

TEMPLATE (SEE INSIDE COVER)

B3 Split facing

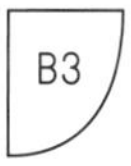

SIZE CHART

	CHEST/BUST	HIP
XS	85 cm (33½ in.)	90 cm (35½ in.)
S	90 cm (35½ in.)	95 cm (37½ in.)
M	95 cm (37½ in.)	100 cm (39½ in.)
L	100 cm (39½ in.)	105 cm (41½ in.)
XL	105 cm (41½ in.)	110 cm (43½ in.)
2XL	110 cm (43½ in.)	118 cm (46½ in.)
3XL	118 cm (46½ in.)	126 cm (49½ in.)
4XL	126 cm (49½ in.)	134 cm (52¾ in.)
5XL	134 cm (52¾ in.)	142 cm (56 in.)
6XL	142 cm (56 in.)	150 cm (59 in.)

CUTTING PLAN

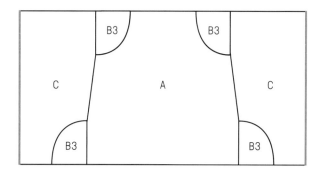

A   Front body

B   Split facing (template B3)

C   Back body

Cutting

	FABRIC WIDTH	FABRIC LENGTH
XS	105 cm (41½ in.)	49 cm (19¼ in.)
S	110 cm (43½ in.)	50 cm (19¾ in.)
M	115 cm (45¼ in.)	51 cm (20 in.)
L	120 cm (47¼ in.)	52 cm (20½ in.)
XL	125 cm (49¼ in.)	53 cm (21 in.)
2XL	130 cm (51 in.)	54 cm (21¼ in.)
3XL	135 cm (53 in.)	55 cm (21¾ in.)
4XL	140 cm (55 in.)	56 cm (22 in.)
5XL	145 cm (57 in.)	57 cm (22½ in.)
6XL	150 cm (59 in.)	58 cm (23 in.)

Referring to the chart above, cut your fabric to the length required for your size and fold it in half widthways, with right sides together.

STEP 2

	A/B WIDTH	C/B WIDTH
XS	24 cm (9½ in.)	24 cm (9½ in.)
S	25.5 cm (10 in.)	25 cm (10 in.)
M	26.5 cm (10½ in.)	26.5 cm (10½ in.)
L	28 cm (11 in.)	27.5 cm (11 in.)
XL	29 cm (11½ in.)	29 cm (11½ in.)
2XL	30.5 cm (12 in.)	30 cm (12 in.)
3XL	31.5 cm (12½ in.)	31.5 cm (12½ in.)
4XL	33 cm (13 in.)	32.5 cm (13 in.)
5XL	34 cm (13½ in.)	34 cm (13½ in.)
6XL	35.5 cm (14 in.)	35 cm (14 in.)

Find the A/B and C/B widths for your size from the chart above. Along the top edge of the fabric, measure the A/B distance from the fold and make a mark. Line up the B3 split facing template in the correct size with this mark and draw around the template. Repeat for the C/B width, this time measuring from the bottom left edge of the fabric. Mark one more straight line to join up the templates from bottom edge to bottom edge. This line becomes the side seam.

1

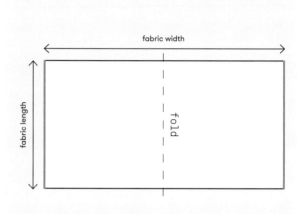

2

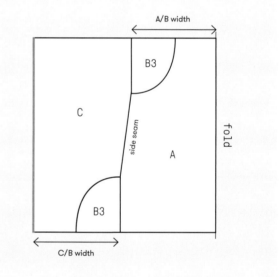

STEP 3   Cut the pieces apart in order from 1 to 3.

STEP 4   Draw in the darts on the sides of the front
body neckline (A). The width and length of
the darts changes depending on the size you
are making:

Sizes XS–L
Width = 3 cm (1¼ in.)
Length = 14 cm (5½ in.)

Sizes XL–6XL
Width = 3.5 cm (1⅜ in.)
Length = 15 cm (6 in.)

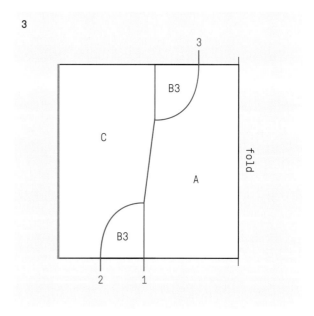

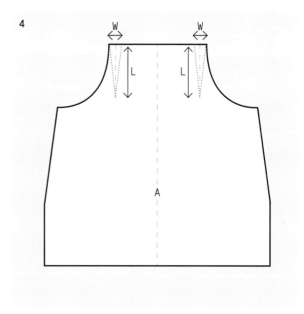

Sewing

1. Centre back seam and darts

STEP 1a   Place the two back pieces (C) right sides together and sew the centre back seam. Overlock (serge) the seam allowances together. Press the seam to one side.

STEP 1b   Sew the darts on the sides of the front neck (A). Press the darts towards the centre front.

2. Attaching the cotton tape and binding

STEP 2a   Attach cotton tape to the armhole edges (see page 18).

STEP 2b   Attach bias binding to the top edges of the front and back (see page 17). Carefully trim off any excess binding on each end.

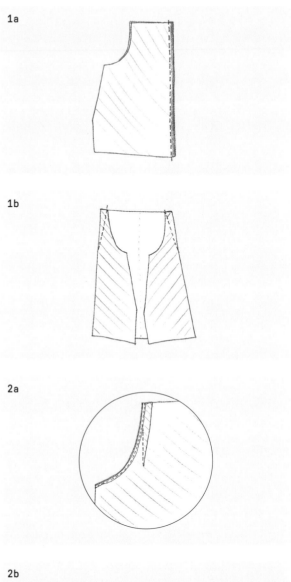

1a

1b

2a

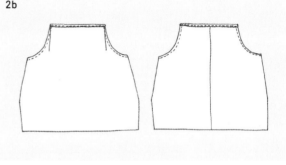

2b

STEP 2c   Attach binding to the underarms on the front and back bodies, leaving a length for the shoulder straps between the front and back necklines (see page 18). Refer to the size chart below for the strap lengths. Make sure that the tape on the inside is covered completely by the binding. After attaching the binding, overlock all four side seams separately.

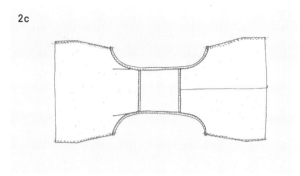

XS	S	M	L	XL	2XL	3XL	4XL	5XL	6XL
15.5 cm	17 cm	18 cm	19.5 cm	20.5 cm	21.5 cm	23 cm	24 cm	25.5 cm	26.5 cm
6 in.	6½ in.	7 in.	7½ in.	8 in.	8½ in.	9 in.	9½ in.	10 in.	10½ in.

TIP   The straps are sewn all in one, so it's a good idea to check before sewing whether the measurements above will suit you. Pin on a scrap strip of bias binding and check what length works for you. As this is made using bias binding, this strap length will stretch out approximately 2–3 cm (¾–1¼ in.) from this measurement after sewing.

3. Side seams, splits and hem

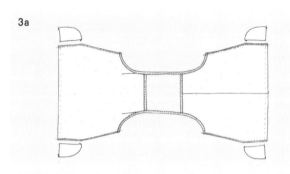

STEP 3a   Press the curved edges of the facing pieces (B3) to the wrong side by 1 cm (⅜ in.).

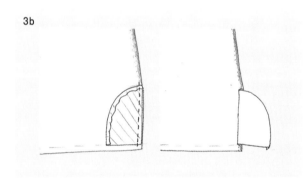

STEP 3b   With right sides together, pin the facing pieces to the side seams of the front and back, approximately 1.5 cm (⅝ in.) up from the hem line. Stitch in place, then press the facings away from the body.

STEP 3c   With right sides together, sew the side seams of the front and back bodies from the underarm to 1 cm (⅜ in.) past the top of the facing.

STEP 3d   Press the seams open and press the facings back so that the wrong sides of the garment and facings are together. Working from the wrong side, stitch the facings down along the curved edge through all layers. Turn up a double 1-cm (⅜-in.) hem and topstitch it in place.

STEP 3e   At the underarms, stitch over the binding on both sides of each side seam to hold the binding down neatly.

Pattern adjustment tips

USING DIFFERENT FABRIC WIDTHS

Place your pattern pieces going the other direction on your fabric, so that the hem and neck are in line with the selvedge and folded edge. This layout requires a centre front seam and the finished length of this singlet is determined by the width of the fabric you are using.

Suitable for all fabric widths.

CHANGES

Add an extra 1 cm (⅜ in.) to the A/B width to account for the centre front seam seam allowance.

3d

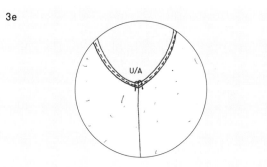

3e

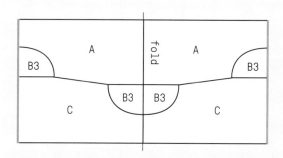

The top panel of this skirt has a slight triangular shape to allow for curve at the hips and the lower panel is gathered. The waist is elasticated.

Skirt

The pattern fits a broad range of fabric widths, as the length of the skirt is determined by the fabric width. This is the only block that does not require any templates to assist with cutting. The skirt comes with 10 size options.

The sample is a size 3XL, made using organic cotton twill 165 cm (65 in.) wide. The waist elastic size has been reduced by 15 cm (6 in.) to accommodate a smaller waist.

SKILL LEVEL ●●○○○

TECHNIQUES USED
Elasticated waist casing (page 20), Gathers (page 21)

PROJECTS
This block is used in the Sun Dress (page 134), Tiered Skirt (page 152), Triangle Skirt (page 158) and Gathered Shirt Dress (page 164).

SUITABLE FABRIC WIDTHS
The recommended widths for all sizes are 135–165 cm (53–65 in.). The narrower your fabric width is, the shorter your skirt will be, so keep this in mind when choosing a fabric.

FABRIC TYPE
Light- to medium-weight linen or cotton (140–200 gsm). This skirt works beautifully in something with a bit of drape that is soft and floaty.

NOTIONS
Elastic 3 cm (1¼ in.) wide for the waist – see the elastic size chart below for cut lengths by size.

(Please note that these are recommended lengths only and you may want to fit elastic to your own measurement.)

XS	S	M	L	XL	2XL	3XL	4XL	5XL	6XL
60 cm	65 cm	70 cm	75 cm	80 cm	85 cm	91 cm	97 cm	103 cm	109 cm
23½ in.	25½ in.	27½ in.	29½ in.	31½ in.	33½ in.	35¾ in.	38 in.	40½ in.	43 in.

SIZE CHART

	WAIST RANGE	MAX. HIP
XS	62–70 cm (24½–27½ in.)	90 cm (35½ in.)
S	67–77 cm (26½–30½ in.)	95 cm (37½ in.)
M	72–82 cm (28½–32½ in.)	100 cm (39½ in.)
L	77–87 cm (30½–34½ in.)	105 cm (41½ in.)
XL	82–92 cm (32½–36½ in.)	110 cm (43½ in.)
2XL	87–97 cm (34½–38½ in.)	118 cm (46½ in.)
3XL	95–105 cm (37½–41½ in.)	126 cm (49½ in.)
4XL	103–113 cm (40½–44½ in.)	134 cm (52½ in.)
5XL	111–121 cm (43½–47½ in.)	142 cm (56 in.)
6XL	119–129 cm (46½–50½ in.)	150 cm (59 in.)

CUTTING PLAN

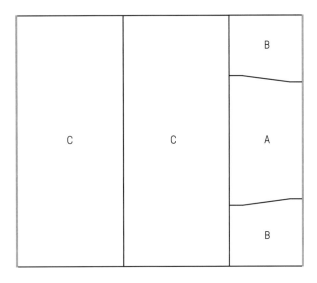

A Front top skirt

B Back top skirt

C Front/back bottom skirt

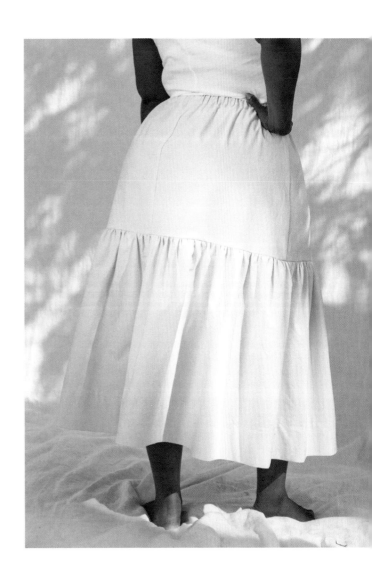

Cutting

STEP 1

	FABRIC LENGTH
XS	112 cm (44 in.)
S	118 cm (46½ in.)
M	124 cm (49 in.)
L	130 cm (51¼ in.)
XL	136 cm (53½ in.)
2XL	142 cm (56 in.)
3XL	148 cm (58¼ in.)
4XL	154 cm (60½ in.)
5XL	160 cm (63 in.)
6XL	166 cm (65½ in.)

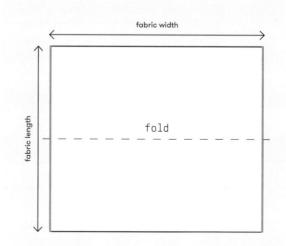

Referring to the chart above, cut your fabric to the length required for your size and fold it in half lengthways, right sides together.

STEP 2

	A WAIST	B WAIST	A/B LENGTH
XS	25 cm (9⅞ in.)	26 cm (10¼ in.)	41 cm (16¼ in.)
S	26.5 cm (10½ in.)	27.5 cm (10⅞ in.)	41.5 cm (16⅜ in.)
M	28 cm (11 in.)	29 cm (11½ in.)	42 cm (16½ in.)
L	29.5 cm (11⅝ in.)	30.5 cm (12 in.)	42.5 cm (16⅝ in.)
XL	31 cm (12¼ in.)	32 cm (12½ in.)	43 cm (16¾ in.)
2XL	32.5 cm (12¾ in.)	33.5 cm (13⅛ in.)	43.5 cm (16⅞ in.)
3XL	34 cm (13⅜ in.)	35 cm (13¾ in.)	44 cm (17 in.)
4XL	35.5 cm (14 in.)	36.5 cm (14⅜ in.)	44.5 cm (17⅛ in.)
5XL	37 cm (14½ in.)	38 cm (15 in.)	45 cm (17¼ in.)
6XL	38.5 cm (15⅛ in.)	39.5 cm (15½ in.)	45.5 cm (17⅜ in.)

C = Equal halves (all sizes)

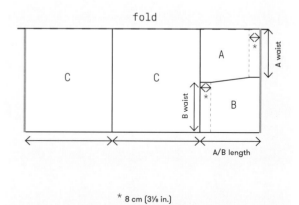

* 8 cm (3⅛ in.)

STEP 2 CONTINUED

Using the chart opposite, find the A/B length and then the A waist and B waist measurements in your size. Measure from the bottom right-hand edge of the fabric inwards, mark your A/B length and draw a vertical line from top to bottom of the fabric.

From the fold, measure down and mark your A waist length on the right-hand edge of the fabric. From the bottom of the vertical A/B line, measure upwards and mark your B waist length. These are your waist points. Draw a **straight** horizontal line 8 cm (3⅛ in.) long from each waist point, then connect these two short lines with a **diagonal** line; this line will be your side seam. Divide the remainder of the fabric into two equal halves for the front/back bottom skirts (C).

STEP 3

Cut the pieces apart in order from 1 to 3.

3

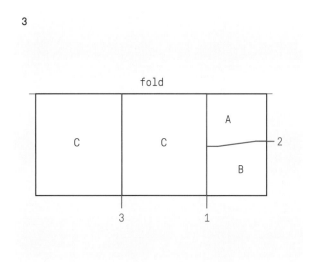

Sewing

1. Side seams and centre back

STEP 1a   With right sides together, sew the centre back seam of the top skirt (B). Overlock (serge) the seam allowances together and press the seam to one side.

STEP 1b   With right sides together, sew the side seams of the front and back top skirts (A + B). Overlock the seam allowances together and press the seams towards the back.

2. Waist casing

STEP 2a   Turn the raw edge of the waist to the wrong side by 1 cm (⅜ in.) and press, then press down a further 3.5 cm (1⅜ in.). Pin in place and stitch close to the bottom of the fold, leaving an opening of around 5 cm (2 in.) at the centre back to thread the elastic through.

STEP 2b   Insert and secure the elastic, following steps 2–5 of Elasticated waist casing on page 20.

3. Gathered panel

STEP 3a   With right sides together, pin and sew the side seams of the front/back bottom skirt panels (C). Overlock the seam allowances together. Press the seams towards the back.

1a

1b

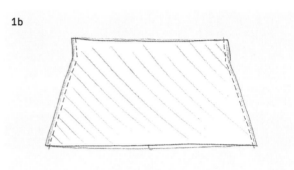

2a

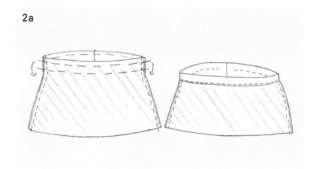

3a

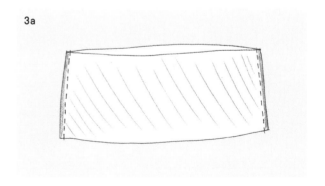

STEP 3b   Gather (see page 21) the top of the panel
           to fit the lower edge of the top skirt pieces
           (A + B).

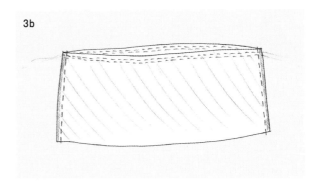

3b

STEP 3c   With right sides together, pin the bottom skirt
           (C) to the top skirt (A + B), making sure that
           the side seams match and that the gathers
           are evenly distributed. Sew the bottom
           skirt to the top skirt and overlock the seam
           allowances together. Press the seam up.

4. Hem

3c

STEP 4   To hem the skirt, turn 1 cm (⅜ in.) to the
           wrong side and press, then try on the skirt
           and turn up the hem to your chosen length.
           Press and pin the hem in place, measuring
           to make sure you have turned up the same
           amount all the way around. Topstitch all
           around.

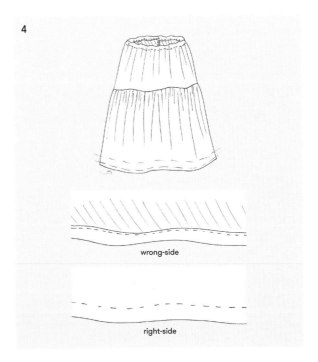

4

wrong-side

right-side

This is a one-size garment where the total body circumference is determined by the width of the fabric you are using.

Shirt

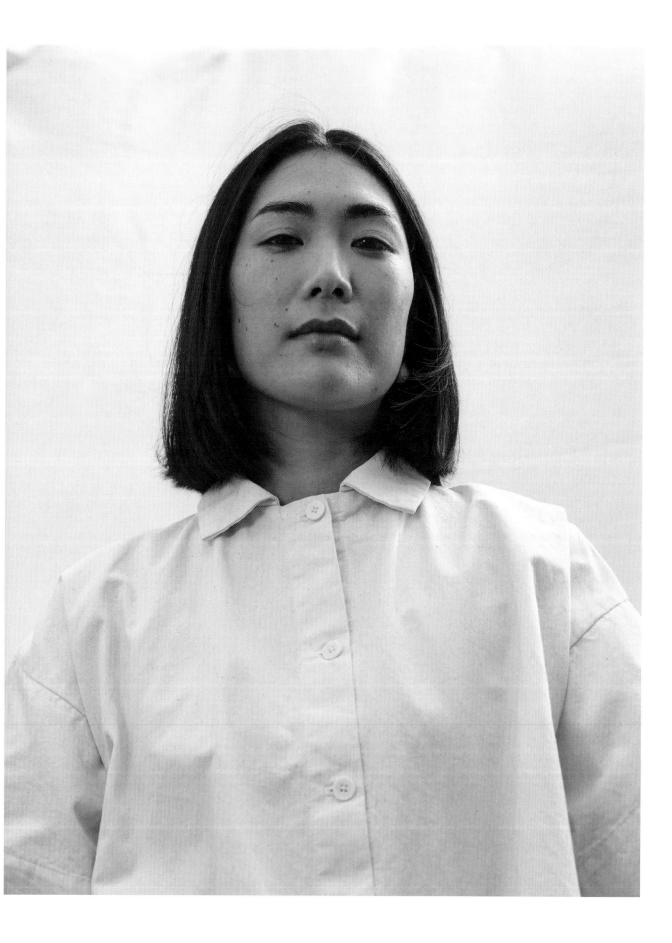

It has short sleeves, a collar, a back pleat and a front closure with buttons and buttonholes. The body length of this garment is easy to alter to your own preference. Tips are included on how to adjust the pattern to size up further.

The sample is made using 145-cm (57-in.) wide organic cotton twill.

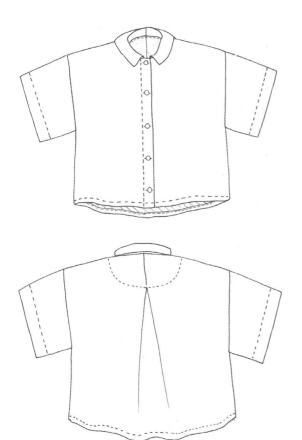

SKILL LEVEL ● ● ● ○ ○

TECHNIQUES USED

Binding (page 15), Inserting a sleeve (page 19), Sewing and attaching a collar and button placket (page 25), Buttons and buttonholes (page 29)

PROJECTS

This block is used in the Gathered Shirt Dress (page 164), Shirt Dress (page 170), Vintage Shirt (page 176)and Quilted Jacket (page 182).

SUITABLE FABRIC WIDTHS

The recommended widths are 135–155 cm (53–61 in.). As this is a one-size garment, the body circumference will get bigger or smaller depending on the fabric width you are using. Check the size chart to see which fabric widths will work for your measurements. If your measurements do not work for the width of fabric you want to use, then refer to Pattern adjustment tips on page 88 for more information.

FABRIC TYPE

Light- to medium-weight linen or cotton (160–220 gsm). This shirt works really nicely in a fabric that has a little bit of structure to it.

NOTIONS

• Binding, 4 cm (1½ in.) wide. You will need two 20-cm (8-in.) lengths and one 45-cm (18-in.) length. The shorter lengths are used to finish the front necklines and the longer length to finish the curve on the back neck facing.

• Five buttons, 1–1.5 cm (⅜–⅝ in.) in diameter, for the front button closure.

• Lightweight iron-on interfacing for the collar and centre front button placket (optional). This is only recommended for very lightweight fabrics or anything that needs a little extra structure added to it. More information on adding interfacing can be found on page 25.

TEMPLATES (SEE INSIDE COVER)

B5 Back neck facing

E Sleeve head curve

SIZE CHART

The size of this garment depends on the width of the fabric you use. This size chart accounts for around 25 cm (10 in.) ease from the actual garment measurements and shows the maximum chest/bust and hip measurement recommended for each fabric width. As this garment is meant to be oversized, you can still work with a wider fabric even if your measurements are a lot smaller than the maximum stated below – see Pattern adjustment tips: Sizing up, page 88. Ideally, however, your measurements should be no more than 25 cm (10 in.) smaller than the maximum shown below.

FABRIC WIDTH	MAX. CHEST/BUST	MAX. HIP
135 cm (53 in.)	96 cm (38 in.)	104 cm (41 in.)
140 cm (55 in.)	101 cm (40 in.)	109 cm (43 in.)
145 cm (57 in.)	106 cm (42 in.)	114 cm (45 in.)
150 cm (59 in.)	111 cm (44 in.)	119 cm (47 in.)
155 cm (61 in.)	116 cm (46 in.)	124 cm (49 in.)

Finished shirt length: 62 cm (24½ in.), measured from shoulder to finished hem. This length can easily be altered on the cutting plan to suit your needs.

Finished sleeve length: When using a 145-cm (57-in.) wide fabric, the sleeve length is approximately 45 cm (17¾ in.), measured from the neck to finished hem. This length varies slightly with different fabric widths and can be altered when turning up the hem.

CUTTING PLAN

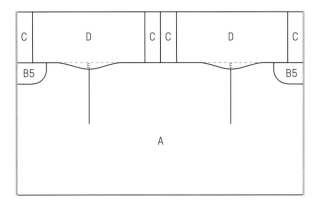

A   Front/back body

B   Back neck facing (template B5)

C   Collar

D   Sleeve

E   Sleeve head curve (template E)

Cutting

STEP 1   Cut the fabric to length (90 cm/35½ in.) and fold it in half widthways, right sides together.

STEP 2   Measure 25 cm (9⅞ in.) down from the top and draw a horizontal line all the way across the fabric. Find the centre point and place the sleeve head curve template (E) along this line, with the curve extending into the front/back body (A). Draw in the sleeve head curve for the sleeve piece (D).

STEP 3   Draw the collar pieces (C) by measuring 9.5 cm (3¾ in.) across from each side edge and drawing a vertical line down from the top edge of the fabric to the horizontal line that you drew in step 2. Place the back neck facing template (B5) on the left-hand edge of the fabric, with the long straight edge on the horizontal line, and draw around it. On the front/back body (A), draw a straight line down from the centre point of the sleeve head curve that is half the width of the sleeve (D) in length for the armhole cut-out.

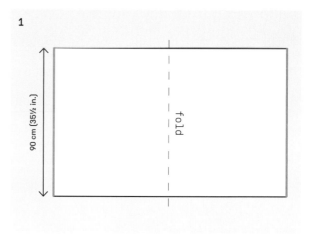

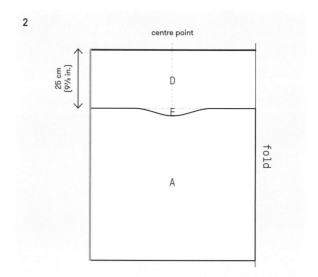

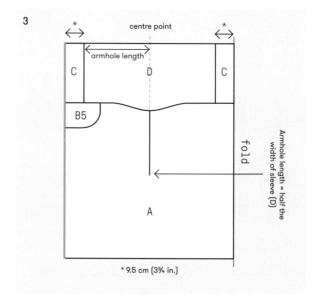

STEP 4   Cut the pieces apart in order from 1 to 6.

STEP 5   Referring to the diagram below, cut one notch 9.5 cm (3¾ in.) away from the centre back fold line (CB) on each side, then two more notches 4.5 cm (1¾ in.) away from the first notches. Then cut one notch 2.5 cm (1 in.) away from the centre front (CF) on each side, another notch 3 cm (1¼ in.) away from the first notch and a third notch 3 cm (1¼ in.) away from the second. Finally, cut a notch at the centre shoulder (SH) points of the sleeves (D).

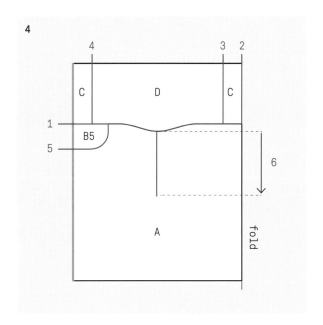

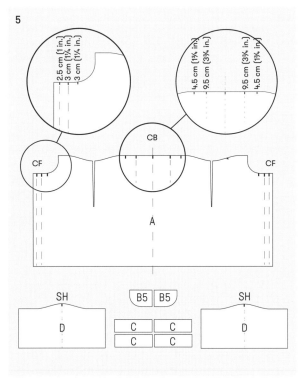

Sewing

1. Centre back pleat

STEP 1 With right sides together, fold the back body in half along the centre back notch line. Lining up the first notches on either side of the centre back line, stitch down from the top for 14 cm (5½ in.). Press the pleat so that the stitch line is in the middle, like an inverted box pleat, and pin it in place. This part will be secured when the back neck facing is attached.

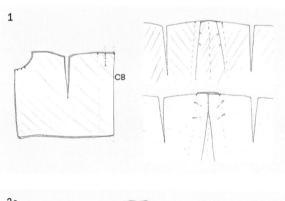

2. Shoulders and sleeves

STEP 2a To create the front sections, with right sides together, fold the left- and right-hand side edges over at the armhole cut-out slits and align the top edges. With right sides together, pin and sew the front and back bodies (D) together at the shoulders. The front neckline edge should match the outermost notch on the back body. Stitch all the way across from one shoulder to the other, stitching across the back neckline and pleat, too. Overlock (serge) the seam allowances together.

STEP 2b With right sides together, pin and sew the underarm seams. Overlock the seam allowances together. Press the seams towards the back of the sleeves.

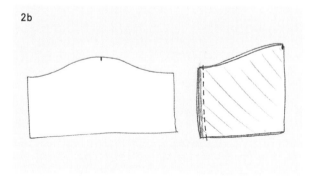

STEP 2c With the garment wrong side out and the sleeves right side out, lift up the centre fronts and slip the sleeves inside the armholes, matching the shoulder notches of the sleeves to the shoulder seams of the body and the underarm seams of the sleeves to the finished point of the armhole cut-out in the body. Pin the sleeves into the armholes. Stitch in place, then overlock the seam allowances together, making sure that the underarm point is finished neatly and is securely stitched without any holes being visible (see page 19).

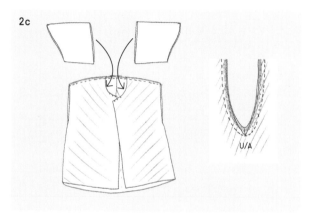

3. Attaching the collar and back neck facing

STEP 3a   Assemble and attach the collar, following steps 1–7 of Sewing and attaching a collar and button placket on pages 25–26.

OPTIONAL   If you are using a very lightweight fabric, you can add a lightweight iron-on interfacing to the wrong side of the collar pieces (i.e. one pair sewn together at the centre back) before you stitch them together.

STEP 3b   With right sides together, stitch the back neck facing pieces (B) together along the centre back seam. Press the seam open. Finish the curved edge of the facing with the longer length of binding (see page 17). Attach the facing to the back neck by following steps 8–12 of Sewing and attaching a collar and button placket on pages 26–27.

4. Front button placket

STEP 4a OPTIONAL   If you are using a lightweight fabric, apply lightweight iron-on interfacing to the centre front edges of the front bodies (A). Fuse all the way along and to the width of the second notch.

STEP 4b   Fold and stitch the button plackets, following steps 13–14 of the Sewing and attaching a collar and button placket on page 28.

3a

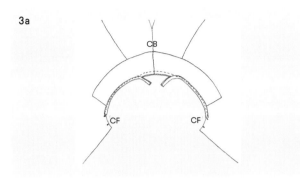

3b

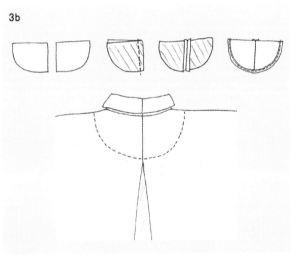

4b

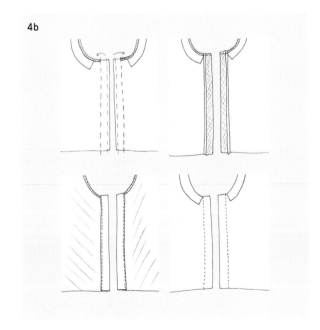

5. Hems and attaching the buttons

5a

STEP 5a   Turn under and press a double 1-cm (⅜-in.) hem around the bottom of the shirt and topstitch in place. Turn under the ends of the sleeves by 1 cm (⅜ in.) and press, then turn up the sleeve hem to your chosen length and press again. Topstitch in place.

STEP 5b   Work five horizontal buttonholes (see page 29) on the right front placket, placing the centre of the top buttonhole about 1.5 cm (⅝ in.) down from the top finished edge and spacing the remaining buttonholes evenly. Make sure that your front button plackets overlap by 3 cm (1¼ in.). Attach buttons to the left placket to correspond.

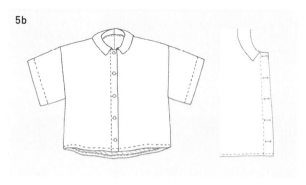

5b

Pattern adjustment tips

SIZING UP

If your fabric width will not allow for a large enough garment for your own measurements, then you can adjust your fabric by adding a strip through the centre of it.

For example, if you have a hip measurement of 140 cm (55 in.) and want to use a fabric that is 155 cm (61 in.) wide, then add a panel to the centre of your fabric that is 30 cm (12 in.) wide. This allows for some extra ease and seam allowance. Make sure your additional panel is not narrower than around 25 cm (10 in.), otherwise it may be difficult to cut your collar pieces correctly at the top.

You should also add a little extra to the length of the body (5 cm/2 in. has been added to the cutting plan on the right but this is easy to adjust yourself).

Do not add length to the sleeves, as this needs to remain the same for the collar pieces to be the correct size. The panel will become a feature seam line on the back body and also on a section of the sleeves. Keep in mind that you may need to adjust the neck size slightly.

Before cutting out your pieces, your fabric should look like this:

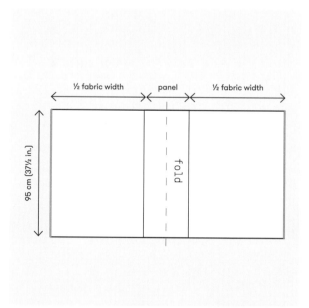

Projects

Fold-back Collar Dress

SKILL LEVEL ●○○○○

BLOCK USED
Tee (page 32)

TECHNIQUES USED
Binding (page 15),
Buttons and buttonholes
(page 29)

This dress, which is made using a square vintage embroidered tablecloth with ready-finished edges, is a very simple modification of the Tee block (page 32). There are no templates for this project and the front collar is created by simply folding back the edges, which means that a section of the underside (the wrong side) of the fabric is visible when the dress is worn.

SIZING

The sample and pattern layout are suitable for sizes S–L. To size up or down, you can use a wider or a narrower fabric.

FABRIC USED

The fabric used for this project is a 130-cm (51-in.) square vintage linen tablecloth with blue embroidery that already has all four edges finished with a turn and turn hem and mitred corners. You can use a piece of fabric cut from the roll instead by finishing all four sides before sewing, but you will need to allow an extra 3.5 cm (1⅜ in.) on each side for this. To finish the edges, fold and press 1 cm (⅜ in.) and then a further 2.5 cm (1 in.) to the wrong side. Mitre the corners and topstitch the hem in place all the way around.

NOTIONS

- Approx. 2 m (2¼ yd) cotton binding, 4 cm (1½ in.) wide, to finish the front sleeves and the front and back hems
- Seven corozo nut buttons, 1 cm (⅜ in.) in diameter

CUTTING PLAN

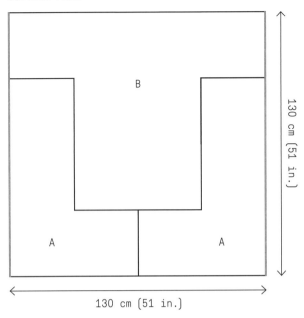

130 cm (51 in.)

130 cm (51 in.)

A Front body

B Back body

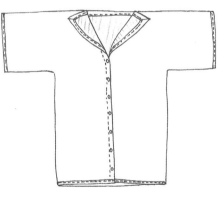

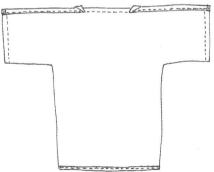

Cutting

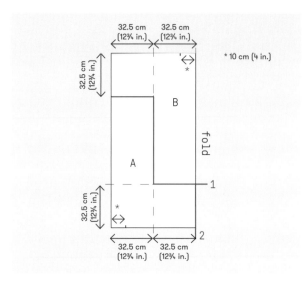

STEP 1   Fold the fabric in half widthways, right sides together.

STEP 2   Prepare to mark out the pattern pieces by dividing the folded fabric into equal-sized squares. Divide it into two equal parts across the width, as in the Tee block (page 38), and into four equal parts along the length, marking the lines with tailor's chalk or a dissolvable fabric marker pen.

STEP 3   Using a dissolvable fabric marker pen, tailor's chalk or a pin, mark the shoulders 10 cm (4 in.) away from the centre back and centre front. Do not cut a notch.

STEP 4   Cut the pieces apart.

Sewing

STEP 1 Bind (see page 17) the hems of the front sleeves.

STEP 2 Overlap the front pieces on top of the back by 2.5 cm (1 in.) at the shoulders and topstitch along the top edge from the sleeve hem to the shoulder mark, 10 cm (4 in.) away from the centre front/centre back on each side.

STEP 3 Fold the garment right sides together, matching the edges, and sew the underarm and side seams in a continuous line of stitching on each side. Snip into the underarm points (see step 2a of the Tee block, page 41), then overlock (serge) the seam allowances together and press the seams towards the back.

STEP 4 Bind the hems all the way around, making sure that the binding at the centre front edges is turned in and finished neatly.

STEP 5 Work seven buttonholes down the right centre front, positioning the first one about 28 cm (11 in.) down from the top of the 'collar' and the last one roughly 12 cm (4¾ in.) up from the hem and spacing the others evenly in between. Sew buttons to the left centre front to correspond (see page 29).

Alternatively, you can omit the buttons and buttonholes and sew the centre front edges together by overlapping them by the width of the centre front 'hem' (2.5 cm/1 in.), and topstitching in the same way as the shoulder seams.

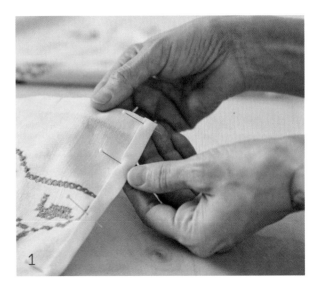

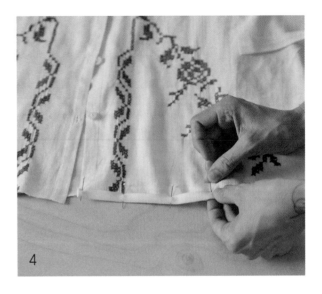

Sweater

SKILL LEVEL ● ○ ○ ○ ○

BLOCK USED
Tee (page 32)

TECHNIQUE USED
Binding (page 15)

This is an oversized, boxy sweater, with a panel added to make long sleeves. A contrast rib finishes the neck.

SIZING

The sample and pattern layout are suitable for sizes XS–M. To size up, you can use a wider fabric or use the alternate layout shown at the end of the Tee block (page 43).

FABRIC USED

Heavyweight cotton jacquard
Width: 120 cm (47 in.)
Length: 110 cm (43 in.)

NOTIONS

- Cotton ribbing, 8 cm (3¼ in.) wide x approx. 44 cm (17½ in.) long, to finish the neck. (Please note some ribbings have more stretch than others, so pin yours on first to check the length you need to cut.)
- Cotton bias binding, 4 cm (1½ in.) wide x 35 cm (14 in.) long, to finish the back neck facing.

TEMPLATE (SEE INSIDE COVER)

B1 Front split facing

CUTTING PLAN

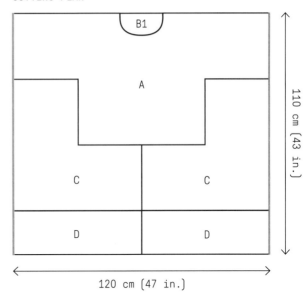

120 cm (47 in.)

110 cm (43 in.)

A   Front body
B   Back neck facing (template B1)
C   Back body
D   Sleeve band

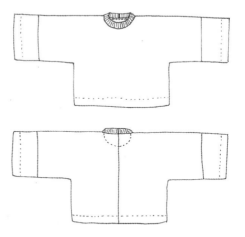

Cutting

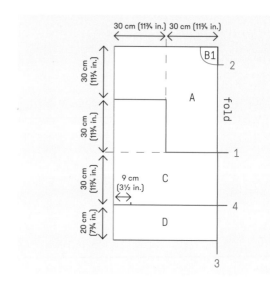

STEP 1   Cut your fabric to length and fold it in half widthways, with right sides together.

STEP 2   Prepare to mark out the pattern pieces by dividing the folded fabric into sections, as shown. Divide it into two equal parts across the width, as in the Tee block (page 38), and into three 30-cm (11¾-in.) and one 20-cm (7¾-in.) section along the length, marking the lines with tailor's chalk or a dissolvable fabric marker pen.

STEP 3   Mark a notch on the back body (C) 9 cm (3½ in.) away from the centre back. Place the B1 template on the fold and draw around it.

STEP 4   Cut the pieces apart in order from 1 to 4.

Sewing

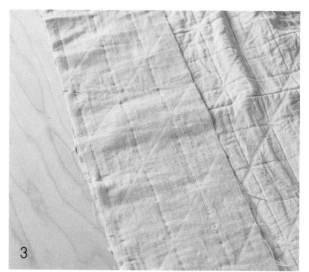

STEP 1   With right sides together, sew the centre back seam. Overlock (serge) the seam allowances together and press the seam to one side.

STEP 2   Pin the front and back pieces right sides together, matching the start of the front neck to the back shoulder notches. Sew the shoulders from the sleeve hem to the shoulder notch on each side. Overlock the seam allowances together and press the seams towards the back.

STEP 3   With right sides together, pin the sleeve bands to the ends of the sleeves and sew them in place. You will need to ease the sleeve bands slightly onto the sleeves. Overlock the seam allowances together, then press the seams down, towards the hem.

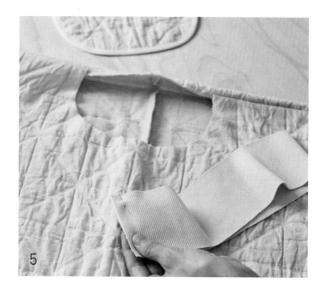

STEP 4 Fold the garment right sides together, matching the edges, and sew the side seams. Snip into the underarm points (see step 2a of the Tee block, page 41), then overlock the seam allowances together and press the seams towards the back.

STEP 5 Fold the neck ribbing in half lengthways, right sides together, and pin and sew the short ends together to form a tube. Press the seam open.

STEP 6 Fold the neck ribbing in half widthways, wrong sides together, and pin the raw edges of the neck ribbing to the right side of the sweater neck, making sure that the ribbing seam matches the centre back seam and that the centre front of the ribbing matches the centre front of the sweater. Sew the ribbing in place, stretching it evenly all the way around. Overlock the seam allowances together and press the seam down.

STEP 7 Bind (see page 17) the curved edge of the back neck facing.

STEP 8 With the **right side of the facing** against the **wrong side of the sweater back** and the curved edge of the facing pointing upwards, pin the straight edge of the back neck facing over the seam allowances of the ribbing and the back of the sweater, making sure that the centre back of the facing lines up with the centre back of the neck/ribbing. Stitch in place.

STEP 9 Press the back neck facing down into the back jumper, wrong side to wrong side. Pin and stitch the facing in place, following the shape of the curved edge.

STEP 10 Overlock the raw edges of the sleeve and body hems and turn up to your chosen length. Press and pin in place. Working from the inside of the garment, hem by hand, using your preferred method.

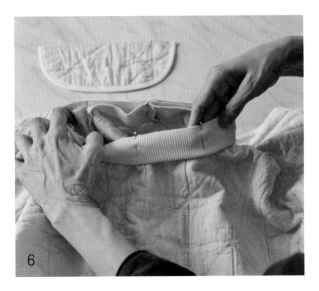

Wrap Top

SKILL LEVEL ●●●○○

BLOCK USED
Tee (page 32)

TECHNIQUE USED
Gathers (page 21)

The wrap top uses the Tee block (page 32) and has a lengthened front bodice, which is achieved by placing the fronts going the other direction on the cutting plan so that the centre front line runs along the bottom edge of the layout. The top has long ties attached to the front that wrap around the body and can be tied in a bow at either the front or the back.

SIZING

This is suitable for sizes XS–XL. It is recommended that you use a fabric at least 145 cm (57 in.) wide.

You can size up the pattern by adding to the cut length and adjusting the measurements:

For sizes 2XL–4XL use a fabric width of 150 cm (59 in.) or above. Add 10 cm (4 in.) to the **first measurement** shown in cutting step 1 and add 10 cm (4 in.) to the total cut length. Add 2.5 cm (1 in.) to all measurements in step 2 of Cutting (page 108).

For sizes 5XL–6XL use a fabric width of 155 cm (61 in.) or above. Add 20 cm (8 in.) to the **first measurement** shown in cutting step 1 and add 20 cm (8 in.) to the total cut length. Add 5 cm (2 in.) to all measurements in step 2 of Cutting (page 108).

When sizing up in this way, your garment will also get longer in the body and sleeve. You can adjust this by making the hem turn-ups deeper.

FABRIC USED

Washed linen, 185 gsm

Width: 145 cm (57 in.)

Length: 110 cm (43 in.)

Choose a fabric that looks good from both the right and the wrong side, as one of the ties (C) will need to be turned around and used with the wrong side of the fabric facing up.

NOTIONS

• Two 15-cm (6-in.) lengths of elastic, 1 cm (⅜ in.) wide, to gather up the side seams.

CUTTING PLAN

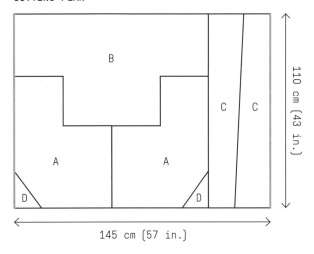

145 cm (57 in.)

110 cm (43 in.)

A Front body

B Back body

C Ties

D Tie extensions

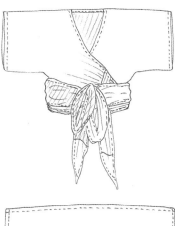

Cutting

STEP 1   Lay out your fabric in a single layer. From the left-hand edge, measure and mark 110 cm (43½ in.) along the top and bottom edges and draw a vertical line down the length of the fabric (line 1). From the bottom of this line, measure and mark a point 15 cm (6 in.) to the right. From the top right-hand edge, measure and mark a point 15 cm (6 in.) to the left. Draw a diagonal line connecting these two points (line 2), then cut along lines 1 and 2 to create your two tie pieces.

STEP 2   Fold the remaining fabric in half widthways, right sides together. Divide the fabric into two equal parts across the width, as in the Tee block (page 38) and four parts along the length, using the measurements in the diagram. Mark out garment pieces A, B and D, then cut along the lines in order from 3 to 5.

Sewing

STEP 1   Flip one of your tie pieces over so that the wrong side of the fabric is facing up and you end up with a symmetrical pair of ties. Stitch the tie extensions (D) to the narrower end of the ties (C) and overlock (serge) the seam allowances together; alternatively, work a French seam.

STEP 2   Gather (see page 21) the centre front edges of the front body pieces to fit the wider end of the ties.

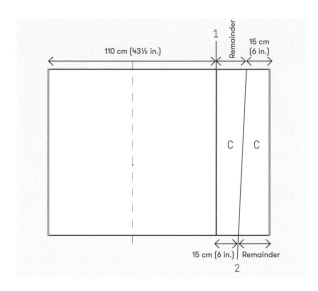

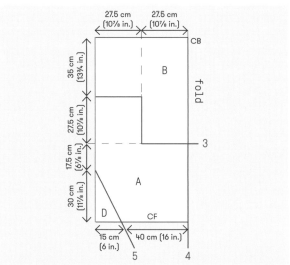

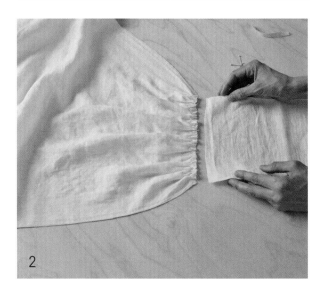

STEP 3 Sew one tie piece to the right side of each front body, making sure that the straight edge of each tie is parallel to the hem line. Overlock the seam allowances together and press the seam allowances away from the body, towards the tie part.

STEP 4 Turn under and press a double 5-mm (¼-in.) hem along the front neckline, tie and tie extension. Stitch all the way along.

STEP 5 Pin the front and back bodies right sides together along the shoulders, starting at the sleeve hems and continuing up to the start of the front necklines on each side. (There will be a gap between the two centre front necklines on the back body – this is your back neckline.) Sew the shoulder seams and then overlock the seam allowances together, continuing the overlocking all the way across the back neckline section as you go.

STEP 6 Press the shoulder seam allowances towards the back; press the back neckline (see step 5) to the wrong side by 1 cm (⅜ in.) as you do so. Stitch all the way along the seam, securing the back neckline as you go.

STEP 7 With right sides together, sew the side seams. Snip into the underarm points (see step 2a of the Tee block, page 41), then overlock the seam allowances together and press the seams towards the back.

STEP 8 Turn under and press a double 5-mm (¼-in.) hem along the hem and the bottom edge of the ties. Stitch all the way along. Make sure the ends of the ties finish in a neat point.

STEP 9 Turn under and press a double 5-mm (¼-in.) hem along the bottom edge of the sleeves, and stitch in place.

STEP 10 Pin a length of elastic to each side seam, stretching it out as you go (10a). Sew in place with either a straight or a zig-zag stitch (10b), so that the elastic gathers up the side seams .

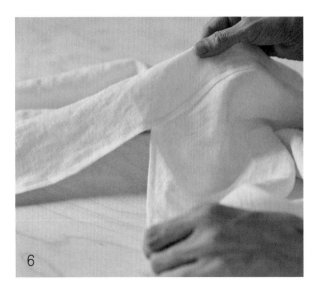

6

8

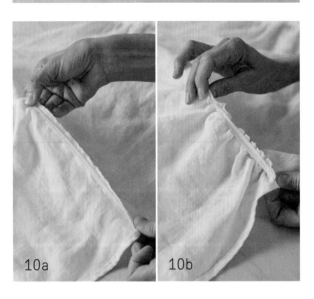

10a 10b

Boiler Suit

BLOCKS USED

Tee (page 32) and
Trouser (page 44)

TECHNIQUES USED

Patch pockets (page 22),
In-seam pockets
(page 23), Elasticated
waist casing (page
20) and Buttons and
buttonholes (page 29)

The boiler suit uses the Tee and Trouser blocks to make a one piece with a button placket at the centre front. It has patch pockets on the chest of the tee and back trousers and in-seam pockets in the trouser side seams. There is black contrast stitching on the patch pockets, on the feature stitching holding down the side-seam pocket bags, on the button plackets and back neck/shoulder seam topstitching, and the topstitching on the sleeve and trouser hems.

SIZING

This sample is a size M.

You can size up by using the full width of the fabric and cutting pieces E, H and I on another piece of fabric. The width of your front and back trouser waist (from side seam to centre front or centre back) is always 1 cm (⅜ in.) wider than the waist of your half bodice. For this layout (size M), the bodice waist measures 30 cm (11¾ in.) and the trouser waist measures 31 cm (12¼ in.).

FABRIC USED

Cotton twill, 8 oz
Width: 150 cm (59 in.)
Length: 180 cm (71 in.)

NOTIONS

• Five corozo nut buttons, 1 cm (⅜ in.) in diameter, for the centre front button placket.

• 75 cm (30 in.) elastic, 1 cm (⅜ in.) wide. (Note: This is for size M; to size up or down, add or subtract 5 cm/2 in. for each size.)

TEMPLATE (SEE INSIDE COVER)

B2 Back patch pocket – remove 10 cm (4 in.) from the top

CUTTING PLAN, SIZE M

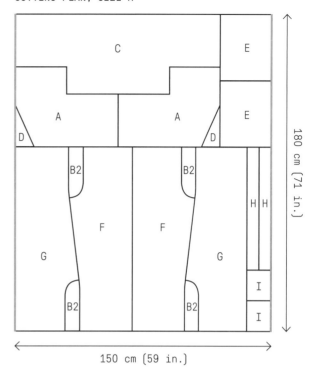

150 cm (59 in.)

180 cm (71 in.)

A Front bodice
B Back patch pocket (template B2, with 10 cm/4 in. removed from the top)
C Back bodice
D Shoulder insert
E Side trouser pocket bag
F Front leg
G Back leg
H Button placket
I Chest patch pocket

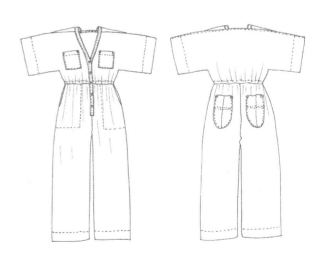

Cutting

The top section is based on the Tee block (page 32), but you cut the pocket bags first before folding the fabric and marking out the remaining pieces. The bottom section is based on the Trouser block (page 44), but you cut the button plackets and chest patch pockets first before folding the fabric in half and marking out the remaining pieces. The back patch pocket template is shortened by 10 cm (4 in.).

STEP 1   Divide your fabric into two pieces by drawing a horizontal line, following the measurements in the diagram, then cut along line 1.

STEP 2   With the top section from step 1 as a single layer, measure 120 cm (47½ in.) across from the left-hand side at the top and bottom and draw a vertical line. Cut along line 2. Divide the small section that you have just cut away into two equal horizontal parts to make the side trouser pocket bags (E), then cut along line 3.

STEP 3   Fold the larger piece of remaining fabric cut from step 2 in half widthways, right sides together. Divide the fabric into two equal parts widthways and three parts lengthways, following the measurements in the diagram. Mark out the front and back bodies (A and C) following the diagram and then cut along lines 4 and 5.

Mark the shoulder inserts (D) on the bottom left corner of the front body by following the measurements on the diagram, measuring 26 cm (10¼ in.) up from the bottom and 8 cm (3¼ in.) across from the left-hand edge, draw a diagonal line joining these points and cut apart along line 6.

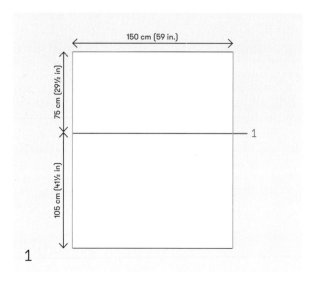

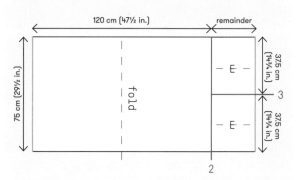

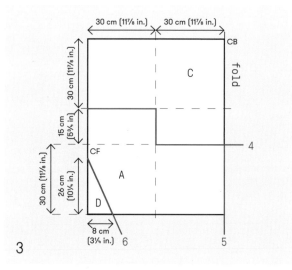

STEP 4 Working with the larger bottom piece of fabric cut in step 1, on the right-hand side measure 14 cm (5½ in.) in from the top and bottom and draw a vertical line down the fabric. Cut along line 7. Measure 70 cm (27½ in.) down from the top of this piece, draw a horizontal line across and cut along line 8. Divide the top cut section vertically into two equal parts to make the button plackets (H) and cut along line 9. Divide the bottom cut section horizontally into two equal parts to make the chest patch pockets (I) and cut along line 10.

STEP 5 Fold the remaining piece cut in step 4 in half widthways, with right sides together, and mark the front and back trouser legs (G and F) and back patch pockets (B2) by following the measurements (this is for a size M). Refer to the Trouser block (page 50) for details of how to cut. Make sure you remove 10 cm (4 in.) from the top of the back patch pocket template (B2) before marking out and cutting. Cut apart in number order along lines 11 to 14.

Mark a notch on the centre front of the trouser legs (F) 20 cm (8 in.) down from the top.

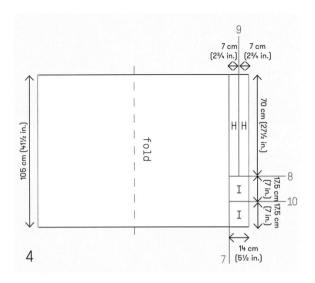

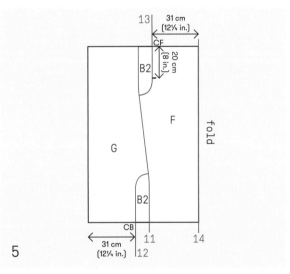

Sewing

STEP 1 Place the front and back bodices (A and C) right sides together and sew the side seams. Snip into the underarm points (see step 2a of the Tee block, page 41), then overlock (serge) the seam allowances together and press the seams towards the back.

STEP 2 Overlock the top edges of the chest patch pockets (I). Press 2.5 cm (1 in.) to the wrong side. Using a contrasting thread, topstitch two rows of stitching along the fold.

STEP 3 Press the side and bottom edges of the chest patch pockets to the wrong side by 1 cm (⅜ in.). Using a contrasting thread, sew them to the front bodices, placing the bottom edge of the pockets 10 cm (4 in.) up from the waist and the centre front edges 7 cm (2¾ in.) in from the centre front of the body.

STEP 4 Prepare the back patch pockets (B2) by following steps 1a and 1b of the Trouser block (page 52). Using a contrasting thread, topstitch the patch pockets to the centre of the back legs, placing the top edge of the pockets 9 cm (3½ in.) down from the waist.

STEP 5 Attach the side trouser pocket bags (E) to the trouser legs (see In-seam pockets, page 23). The pocket opening should measure 15 cm (6 in.). Topstitch down the side and bottom edges of the pockets to the trouser legs with a contrasting thread so that the stitching is visible on the right side of the garment.

STEP 6 Pin the front legs (F) right sides together. Starting from the notch, sew the crotch seam. Overlock the seam allowances together and press the seam to one side.

STEP 7 Sew the centre back, side and inside leg seams, following steps 2a, 2b and 2d of the Trouser block (page 52). Overlock the seam allowances together. Press the side seams towards the back. Press the front crotch seam in the opposite direction to the back crotch seam, to reduce bulk.

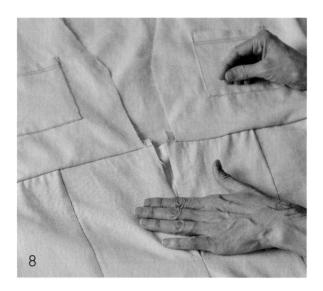

8

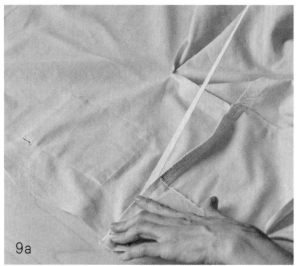

9a

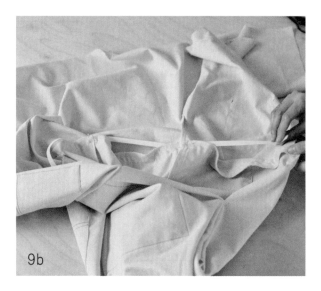

9b

STEP 8   With right sides together, matching the side seams and taking a 2-cm (¾-in.) seam allowance, sew the bodice waist to the trouser waist. Note that the centre front edges of the trouser will extend beyond the centre front of the bodice by 1 cm (⅜ in.). Overlock the seam allowances together. Press the seam up.

STEP 9   Starting at one side seam, pin elastic to the waist seam (9a) at the centre front, side seams and centre back, making sure that the elastic is stretched evenly between these four points (9b) and that it is sitting underneath the pressed-up waist seam allowance. Stitch the waist seam allowance down, working from the wrong side of the garment, making sure that you encase the elastic in as you go.

STEP 10   The longest edge of the shoulder insert (D) is the edge cut on the diagonal of the fabric, which follows the angle of the neckline cut out from the front bodice piece (10a). With right sides together, pin this edge to the front shoulder and sew together (10b). Overlock the seam allowances together. Press the seams towards the back.

STEP 11   With right sides together, placing one raw edge of the placket level with the edge of the raw bodice, pin and sew one side of each button placket to the front bodice and trouser (11a and 11b). (Note that the centre front edge of the trouser extends 1 cm/⅜ in. beyond the bodice, so this part of the placket will be 1 cm/⅜ in. away from the raw edge of the centre front trouser.) Sew from the top of the placket to 1 cm (⅜ in.) past the start of the centre front crotch seam, leaving the bottom part of the placket (approximately 2.5 cm/1 in.) loose. This effectively means that you're taking a 1-cm (⅜-in.) seam allowance on the bodice section and a 2-cm (¾-in.) seam allowance on the centre front trouser.

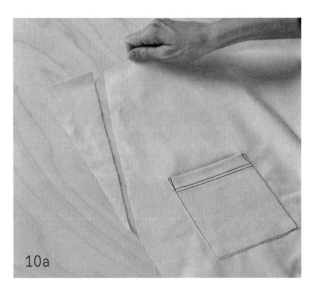

10a

10b

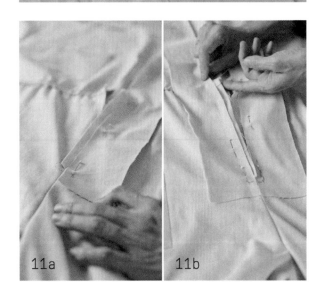

11a   11b

STEP 12   Snip into the centre front crotch seam
           allowances at a right angle, right up to the
           final stitch point of the placket on each side.

STEP 13   Along the raw edge of each placket, fold and
           press 1 cm (⅜ in.) to the wrong side, then
           press the plackets in half, to the inside of
           the garment, and pin in place. Topstitch the
           plackets in place, making sure that you catch
           in the undersides of the plackets as you go.
           Work a second line of topstitching on the
           outer edges of the plackets.

STEP 14   Overlap the bottom of the plackets so that
           they line up neatly and fit into the section
           at the bottom that has been snipped into.
           Turn the unstitched section of the plackets'
           seam allowances to the wrong side as far as
           the stitching at the start of the centre front
           crotch seam (14a). Working from the inside
           of the garment, sew the bottom edge of this
           seam, right sides together, to the bottom of
           the button placket, then overlock the bottom
           edges of the button plackets together to
           finish neatly (14b).

TIP   Leave a little tail of overlocking on each end
           which you can then tuck under and stitch
           down, otherwise the overlocking may come
           undone.

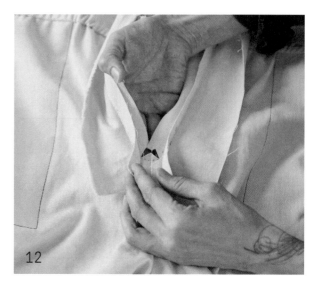

12

13

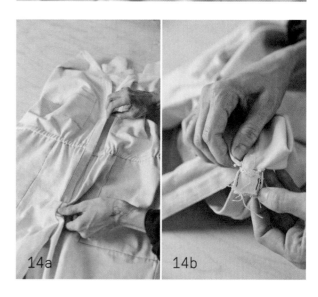

14a   14b

STEP 15 With right sides together, starting at the sleeve hems and continuing up to the start of the front necklines on each side, pin the shoulder inserts/front bodice shoulders to the shoulders of the back bodice. (There will be a gap between the two centre front necklines on the back body – this is your back neckline.) Sew the shoulder seams and then overlock the seam allowances together, continuing the overlocking all the way across the back neckline section as you go. Press the shoulder seam allowances towards the back; press the back neckline to the wrong side by 1 cm (⅜ in.) as you do so. Topstitch all the way along the seam in a contrasting thread, securing the back neckline as you do so. If you wish, you can add a second row of contrasting topstitching on the back neck, between the shoulder points, as a decorative feature, as shown here.

STEP 16 Turn the sleeve and trouser hems to the wrong side by 1 cm (⅜ in.), then turn up the hems to your chosen length and pin and topstitch in place using a contrasting thread.

STEP 17 Add buttons and vertical buttonholes (see page 29) to the button plackets. Position the first button at the waist seam and then add two above and two below, approximately 7 cm (2¾ in.) apart.

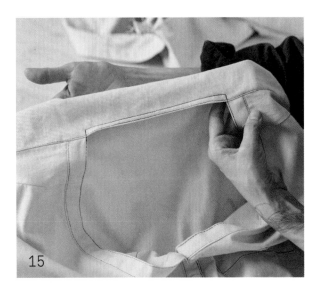

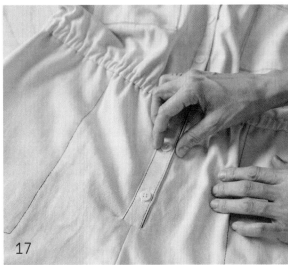

Shorts

SKILL LEVEL ●●○○○

BLOCK USED
Trouser (page 44)

TECHNIQUES USED
Elasticated waist casing
(page 20), Patch pockets
(page 22)

This is a shortened version of the Trouser block, with belt loops and a waist tie. The side seams are eliminated from this pattern and the height of the B2 template is reduced slightly so that the waist sits slightly lower.

SIZING

The pattern layout is for a size 4XL.

To size up or down, make the following adjustments:

1   Determine the total fabric length by finding your waist/pocket width from the Trouser block (page 50) and multiplying this by 2.

2   Add or remove 1 cm (⅜ in.) to the length per size (see Cutting, step 1, page 124).

FABRIC USED

Washed linen, 185 gsm

Width: 145 cm (57 in.)

Length: Trouser block waist/pocket length for your size x 2

NOTIONS

• Elastic, 5 cm (2 in.) wide.
  Refer to the elastic size chart for the Trouser block (page 46) and add a little extra to accommodate the shorts sitting slightly lower on your waist.

TEMPLATE (SEE INSIDE COVER)

B2 Back pocket – remove 2.5 cm (1 in.) from the top

CUTTING PLAN, SIZE 4XL

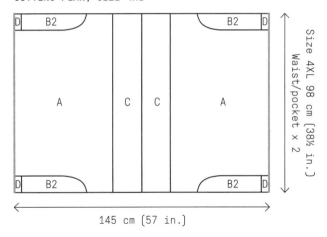

145 cm (57 in.)

Size 4XL 98 cm (38½ in.)
Waist/pocket x 2

A   Front/back leg

B   Back pocket (template B2 – remove 2.5 cm/1 in. from top of template)

C   Waist tie

D   Belt loops

Cutting

STEP 1   Fold the fabric in half widthways, right sides together. Mark out the front/back leg (A), belt loops (D) and back pockets (B2). The remaining fabric is for the waist ties (C).

STEP 2   Cut along the lines in order from 1 to 6.

Sewing

These shorts are made with French seams, but you can sew a normal seam and overlock (serge) to finish the seams instead.

STEP 1   Following step 1 of the Trouser block (see page 52), sew and attach the patch pockets to the back legs of the shorts, positioning them 18 cm (7 in.) down from the waist.

STEP 2   Place the front and back legs right sides together and sew the crotch seams with a French seam. Press the seams towards the left front on the front shorts and towards the right back on the back shorts, so that the seams will be offset when you sew the inside leg seams in step 3.

STEP 3   Sew the inside leg seams with a French seam. Press the seams towards the back. Turn the shorts right side out.

STEP 4   Following step 3 of the Trouser block (see page 53), sew the waist casing and insert the elastic.

STEP 5   Turn in the long ends of the belt loops by 1 cm (⅜ in.) and press, then fold down the middle and press in half lengthways. Topstitch the ends together. Topstitch along both long edges. Press under the short ends of the belt loops by approximately 1 cm (⅜ in.) and pin to the shorts, positioning one on each side of the front near the side seam and one on each side of the centre back. Topstitch the belt loops securely to the waist casing.

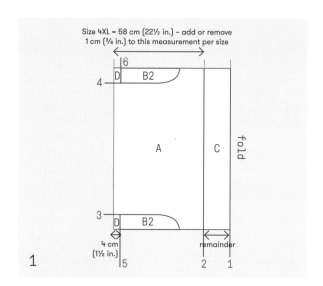

Size 4XL = 58 cm (22½ in.) – add or remove 1 cm (⅜ in.) to this measurement per size

STEP 6   At the bottom of the legs, turn 1 cm (⅜ in.) to the wrong side and press. Turn up the hem to your chosen length and press and pin in place. Topstitch close to the fold.

STEP 7   With right sides together, sew the centre back seam of the waist ties. Press the seam open. Fold the waist tie in half widthways, right sides together, and stitch all around, leaving a 10-cm (4-in.) opening at the centre back. Depending on the shorts size you have cut, you may need to take a larger seam allowance than normal to make the waist tie narrower. The finished width of the tie should be 8–12 cm (3–4¾ in.).

STEP 8   Turn the waist tie right side out and press. Turn under the raw edges at the opening and slipstitch the gap closed.

STEP 9   Thread the waist tie through the belt loops.

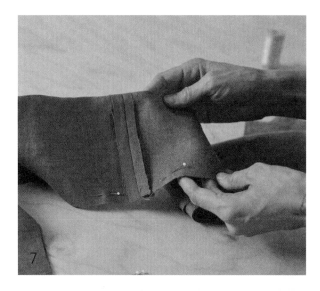

Playsuit

SKILL LEVEL ●●●●○

BLOCKS USED
Singlet (page 56) and Trouser (page 44)

TECHNIQUES USED
Underarm tape (page 18), In-seam pockets (page 23)

The playsuit combines the Singlet and Trouser blocks to make a one-piece garment. The straps are made from contrast bias strips that are sandwiched between the front/back bodies and facings and then tied at the shoulder in a bow. There are in-seam pockets and a waist tie for shaping. Unlike the Singlet block, there are no darts in the front bodice. The length of the playsuit is determined by the width of your fabric.

SIZING

The sample and pattern layout are a size S.

To size up or down, make the following adjustments:

1   Determine the total fabric length by finding your waist/pocket width from the Trouser block (page 50) and multiplying it by 4.

2   For each size difference, add or remove 3 mm (⅛ in.) from the width of the neckline on the front and back bodice and the front and back facing pieces A, C, D and E (shown as lines 4 and 7 in the cutting steps).

FABRIC USED

Re-purposed second-hand curtains, heavyweight textured cotton/linen blend

Width: 150 cm (59 in.)

Length: Trouser waist/pocket length x 4

NOTIONS

• Natural linen bias strips, 2.5 cm (1 in.) wide, to make rouleau ties for the straps. Cut four strips 60 cm (24 in.) long.

• Cotton tape, 8 mm (⁵⁄₁₆ in.) wide for the underarms. See the Singlet block for the size chart and add an extra 2.5 cm (1 in.) to the measurement in your size for each underarm. Cut four lengths. Size S = 4 × 26 cm (10¼ in.).

TEMPLATES (SEE INSIDE COVER)

B2 Waist tie; template B2 is added to piece F at the marking-out stage to create long waist ties

B3 Pocket bag

CUTTING PLAN, SIZE S

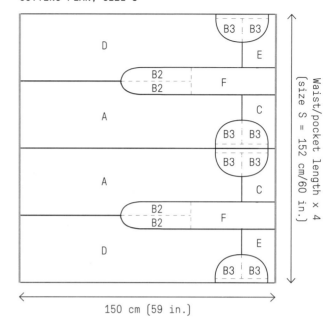

Waist/pocket length × 4
(size S = 152 cm/60 in.)

150 cm (59 in.)

A   Front body   D   Back body

B   Pocket bag   E   Back facing

C   Front facing   F   Waist tie (template B2)

Cutting

STEP 1   Fold the fabric in half lengthways, right sides together. Referring to the Singlet and Trouser block cutting plans and following the dimensions on the diagram, mark out the pattern pieces.

Note: The cutting plan gives the measurements for size S. If you're making a smaller size, remove 3 mm (⅛ in.) per size from the front and back body neck widths (the points marked with an asterisk, lines 4 and 7). If you're making a larger size, add 3 mm (⅛ in.) per size at these points.

STEP 2   Cut along the lines in order from 1 to 7.

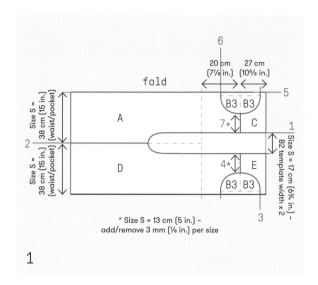

Sewing

STEP 1   Place the front body pieces (A) right sides together and sew the centre front seam. Overlock (serge) the seam allowances together. Press the seam to one side. Repeat with the back body pieces (D).

STEP 2   Place the pocket bags (B3) right sides together in pairs. Sew together along the curved edge. Overlock the seam allowances together.

STEP 3   Referring to In-seam pockets (page 23), attach the pocket bags to the side seams of the front bodies, with the pocket opening starting 18 cm (7 in.) down from the underarm (3a). On the pocket bag the opening should begin around 1.5 cm (⅝ in.) down from the top overlocked seam and the opening should measure 15 cm (6 in.) in length (3b).

STEP 4   Overlock the centre front seam allowances of the front facings separately. Place the front facings (C) right sides together and sew the centre front seam. Press the seam open. Repeat with the back facings (E).

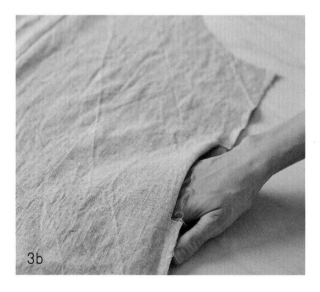

STEP 5 Overlock the bottom edges of the front and back facing pieces.

STEP 6 Attach cotton tape to the curved armhole edges of the front and back facings (see page 18), on the wrong side of the fabric.

STEP 7 Place the front body and front facing right sides together. Using a 5-mm (¼-in.) seam allowance, sew the curved underarm seams. Repeat with the back body and back facing pieces.

STEP 8 Press the seams towards the facings and understitch to hold the facings neatly in place.

STEP 9 Make four rouleau loops using the pre-cut lengths of 2.5-cm (1-in.) bias binding. Fold each strip in half widthways, right sides together. Sew together all the way along, stitching no more than 8 mm (⁵⁄₁₆ in.) from the folded edge. Turn the rouleau loops right side out using a loop turner. Alternatively, thread a thick sewing needle with a length of strong thread, then attach it securely to one end of the sewn loop and feed the needle all the way through the inside of the loop and out the other end of the loop. Gently pull the thread to turn the loop right side out. Tie a knot at one end of each strap and neatly trim off any excess.

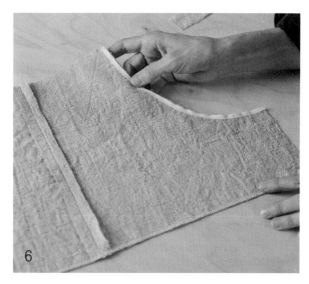

10

STEP 10   Lift up the facings and pin the un-knotted ends of the straps to the top edges of the front and back bodies; the straps should sit flush up against the armhole seams on the left and right of the front and back neck. Pin the top edge of the facing to the top edge of the body neckline, so that the straps are sandwiched in between, making sure that the underarm seam allowances are turned down neatly into the facing side on each end. Using a 1-cm (⅜-in.) seam allowance, stitch all the way across the top edges. Press the seams towards the facing. On the facing side, understitch as far as you can between the straps to hold the seam down neatly.

STEP 11   Place the front and back bodies right sides together. Lift up the facings so they're also right sides together and pin all the way down the side seams, from the top edge of the facings (this will be the bottom edge when the facings are folded back down) right down to the bottom edge of the bodies. Stitch the side seams in one continuous line of stitching on each side. Take a wider seam allowance starting from the top of the underarm if required, making sure that you take the same amount from the facing side seam as you do the body (this layout makes for a larger bodice width, so you may want to bring this in slightly). Overlock the seam allowances together. Press the seams towards the back.

TIP   Make sure that the underarm seams of the front and back bodies match and that the pocket bags are caught neatly and the pocket bag openings are kept free.

STEP 12   Turn the facing to the inside of the garment, so that the wrong sides of garment and facing are together. Press the facing down neatly all the way around and then secure the bottom edges of the facings to the inside of the body side seams with a few hand stitches.

STEP 13   With right sides together, sew the inside leg seams. Overlock the seam allowances together. Press the seams towards the back.

STEP 14 Overlock the bottom edge of the legs. Turn the garment right side out, then press the hems up to your chosen length. Topstitch in place.

STEP 15 Place the waist ties right sides together and sew the centre back seam. Press the seam open.

STEP 16 Fold the waist tie in half widthways, right sides together, and stitch all around, leaving a 10-cm (4-in.) opening at the centre back.

STEP 17 Turn the waist tie right side out and press. Turn under the raw edges of the opening and slipstitch the gap closed.

STEP 18 Matching the centre back seams, pin the waist tie to the body at the desired waist height and stitch it in place, stitching across the tie from top to bottom so that it's firmly attached to the garment. Wrap around the waist and tie at the front.

Sun Dress

SKILL LEVEL ●●○○○

BLOCKS USED
Singlet (page 56) and
Skirt (page 68)

TECHNIQUES USED
Underarm tape (page
18), Binding (page 15),
Gathers (page 21)

The sun dress combines a cropped version of the Singlet block with the gathered panels from the Skirt block. It has side splits on the hem, which are faced in the same way as the Singlet, and black bias binding is used to form the straps and to finish the neckline and armholes. The length of the dress is determined by the width of the fabric you are using.

SIZING

This sample is a size S.

To size up or down, make the following adjustments:

• Add/remove 5 cm (2 in.) to the total fabric length per size.

• Add/remove 3 mm (⅛ in.) to the bodice length per size (see Cutting step 1, page 138).

• The length of the dress is determined by the width of your fabric.

FABRIC USED

Organic cotton gingham, 160 gsm

Width: 165 cm (65 in.)

Length: 106 cm (41¾ in.)

NOTIONS

• Cotton tape, 8 mm (⁵⁄₁₆ in.) wide, for the front and back underarms. See the Singlet block for the size chart (page 58) and add an extra 1 cm (⅜ in.) to the measurement for your size for each underarm; cut four lengths. Size S = 24.5 cm (9⅝ in.).

• Organic cotton bias binding, 4 cm (1½ in.) wide, to finish the neck and underarms/straps. See the Singlet block for the size charts. Add an extra 2 cm (¾ in.) to the measurement for your size for each of the underarm/strap lengths and cut two lengths. Size S = 64 cm (25½ in.). The front and back neck bindings should stay the same as the Singlet block chart in your size (page 59); cut two lengths. Size S = 22 cm (8½ in.).

TEMPLATE (SEE INSIDE COVER)

B3 Split facing

CUTTING PLAN, SIZE S

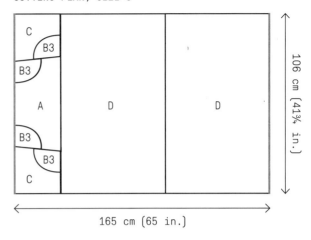

106 cm (41¾ in.)

165 cm (65 in.)

A   Front bodice

B   Split facing (template B3)

C   Back bodice

D   Front/back skirt

Cutting

STEP 1 Calculate the total length of fabric you require (see Sizing, page 135, for details of how to size up or down). Fold the fabric in half lengthways, right sides together. From the left-hand selvedge, measure and mark 30 cm (12 in.) across the fold. The measurement shown in this diagram is for a size S; to size up or down, adjust this measurement by 3 mm (⅛ in.) per size. Draw a vertical line down from this point. Divide the rest of the fabric evenly across the width and draw another vertical line to make your front and back skirt pieces (D). Cut along lines in order from 1 to 2.

STEP 2 Working with the left-hand section that you cut off in step 1, with the fabric still folded, measure and mark your A/B and C/B widths by referring to the diagram. The measurements shown in this diagram are for a size S; to size up or down, refer to your measurements in the size chart of the Singlet block (page 59).

STEP 3 Draw a line across the fabric connecting the A/B and C/B points. Place the B3 template on the fabric according to the diagram, lining up the straight edge of the template with the left and right vertical edges of the fabric. Draw around the curved edge of the template and extend this line past the template to connect it up to the diagonal line already drawn; this will add around 1cm (⅜ in.) to the side seams of the front and back bodies. Cut along the lines in order from 3 to 5.

STEP 4 Open out the front body piece (A). On the wrong side of the fabric, mark the darts on the top side neck edges using the measurements in the Singlet block (page 63).

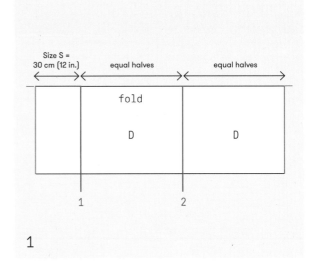

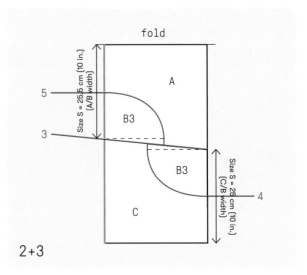

Sewing

STEP 1 — Following steps 1 and 2 of the Singlet block, sew the centre back seam on the back bodice (C) and the neck darts in the front bodice (A). Attach cotton tape to the underarms (see page 18). Attach bias binding to the neckline and underarms, creating the shoulder straps in the process (see page 17).

STEP 2 — With right sides together, sew the bodice side seams. Overlock (serge) the seam allowances together and press the seams towards the back. At the underarms, topstitch over the binding to hold it down neatly.

STEP 3 — Overlock the side edges of the front and back skirt pieces (D) separately, as one layer of fabric.

STEP 4 — Following steps 3a and 3b of the Singlet block, prepare the side split facings and attach them to the front and back skirts, approximately 1 cm (⅜ in.) up from the hem edge.

STEP 5 — Following step 3c of the Singlet block, with right sides together, sew the side seams of the skirt from the waist down to around 1 cm (⅜ in.) past the top of the facings.

STEP 6 — Press the seams open and press the facings back so that the wrong sides of the garment and facings are together. Working from the wrong side, stitch the facings down following the curved edge all the way around.

STEP 7 — Turn up and press a double 1-cm (⅜-in.) hem and stitch it in place.

STEP 8 — Gather (see page 21) the top of the skirt to fit the bottom edge of the bodice.

STEP 9 — With right sides together, matching the side seams, sew the skirt to the bodice. Overlock the seam allowances together. Press the seam up.

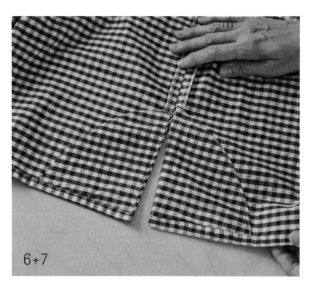

6+7

9

Patchwork Singlet

SKILL LEVEL ●●○○○

BLOCK USED
Singlet (page 56)

TECHNIQUES USED
Underarm tape (page 18), Binding (page 15)

This is a cropped version of the Singlet block that is patchworked together using offcuts from other projects. Instead of the B3 pieces being used to make side splits, they are used to cover the seams on the inside, which makes a detailed curved stitch line visible on the outside of the garment.

SIZING

This sample is a size M.

To size up or down make the following adjustments:

• Add/remove 5 cm (2 in.) to the total fabric width per size and use the A/B and C/B widths from the Singlet block for your chosen size.

• Add/remove 1 cm (⅜ in.) to the bodice length per size.

FABRIC USED

Linen remnants saved from other projects patchworked into one larger piece. These measurements are suitable for a size M.

Width: 111 cm (43¾ in.)

Length: 38 cm (15 in.)

NOTIONS

• Cotton tape, 8 mm (⁵⁄₁₆ in.) wide for the front and back underarms. See the Singlet block for the size chart (page 58) and add an extra 1 cm (⅜ in.) to the measurement for your size for each underarm; cut four lengths. Size M = 4 × 25.5 cm (10 in.).

• Organic cotton bias binding, 4 cm (1½ in.) wide, to finish the neck and underarms and straps. See the Singlet block for the size charts (page 59). For the underarm/ strap lengths, add an extra 2 cm (3/4 in.) to the measurement for your size; cut two lengths. Size M = 67 cm (26¼ in.). The front and back neck bindings should stay the same as the Singlet block chart in your size; cut two lengths. Size M = 23 cm (9 in.).

TEMPLATE (SEE INSIDE COVER)

B3 Split facing

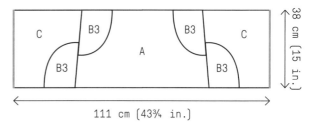

A   Front body

B   Side seam facing (template B3)

C   Back body

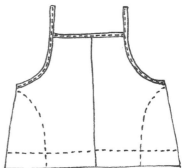

Cutting

STEP 1 Calculate the total length of fabric you require (1a) – see Sizing, page 141, for details of how to size up or down. Using 1-cm (⅜-in.) seam allowances, patchwork square pieces of fabric together to reach the desired width and length (1b); this sample was made using nine even-sized squares across the width and three down the length. Once you have sewn the three individual rows, press the seams in opposite directions on alternate rows to reduce bulk.

1a

STEP 2 Fold the patchworked fabric in half widthways, right sides together. Referring to the chart in the Singlet block and the diagram, measure and mark your A/B width along the top right of the fabric and your C/B width along the bottom left. This diagram shows the measurements for a size M.

Draw a line from top to bottom of the fabric, connecting the A/B and C/B points. Place the B3 template on the fabric according to the diagram, lining up the straight edge of the template with the top and bottom horizontal edges of the fabric. Draw around the curved edge of the template and extend this line past the template to connect it up to the diagonal line already drawn; this will add around 1 cm (⅜ in.) to the side seams of the front and back bodies. Cut along the lines in order from 1 to 3.

1b

STEP 3 Open out the front body piece (C). On the wrong side of the fabric, mark the darts on the top side neck edges using the measurements in the Singlet block (page 63).

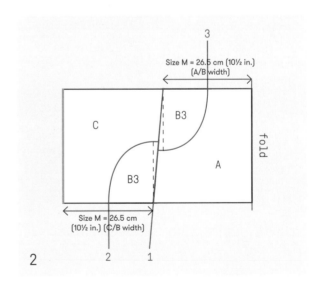

2

Size M = 26.5 cm (10½ in.) (A/B width)

3

B3

C

B3

A

fold

Size M = 26.5 cm (10½ in.) (C/B width)

2   1

Sewing

STEP 1 Following steps 1 and 2 of the Singlet block, sew the centre back seam on the back bodice (C) and the neck darts in the front bodice (A). Attach cotton tape to the underarms (see page 18). Attach bias binding to the neckline and underarms, creating the shoulder straps in the process (see page 17).

STEP 2 With right sides together, sew the bodice side seams. Press the seams open.

STEP 3 Place the facings right sides together, in pairs. Pin and sew them together along one short edge to create two semi-circular pieces. Press the seams open. Overlock (serge) the curved edge of each facing.

STEP 4 Matching the facing seams to the side seams and starting just below the underarm binding, pin the facings on the wrong side of the bodice, wrong sides to wrong sides.

STEP 5 Working from the wrong side, stitch the facings in place, following the curved edge all the way around.

STEP 6 Overlock the hem and press it up so that it covers the bottom edge of the facings. Topstitch the hem in place.

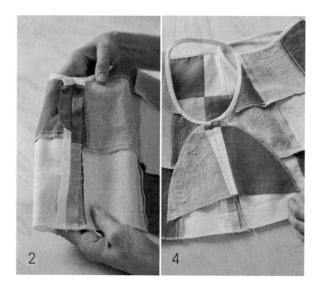

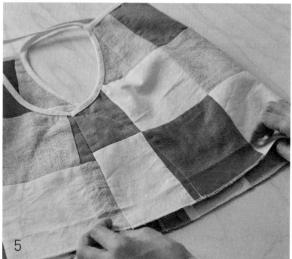

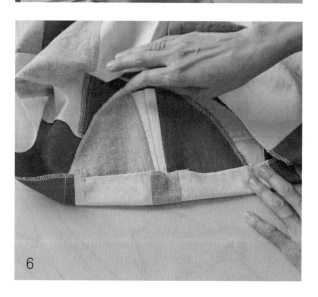

Slip Dress

SKILL LEVEL ●●○○○

BLOCK USED
Singlet (page 56)

TECHNIQUES USED
Underarm tape (page 18),
Binding (page 15)

The slip dress is a simple adjustment to the Singlet block, adding length and longer splits. This dress is made from a vintage tablecloth, and the top and bottom edges of the tablecloth are used as the finished hem edges. The neck and armholes are finished with contrasting white binding, which also forms the straps.

SIZING

This sample is a size L.

Made using a vintage tablecloth, this same size piece of fabric can accommodate a size range of XS–2XL, with the side seam angle changing slightly depending on what size you are cutting. To size up further, use a wider fabric or change the direction of your pattern piece so that the hems and top neck edges line up with the selvedges. With this option, your fabric width will determine the garment length.

To size up or down, make the following adjustments:

- Use the A/B and C/B widths from the Singlet block for your chosen size.

FABRIC USED

Re-purposed vintage tablecloth in a medium-weight linen.

Width: 150 cm (59 in.)

Length: 125 cm (49 in.)

NOTIONS

- Cotton tape, 8 mm (⁵/₁₆ in.) wide, for the underarms. See the Singlet block for the size chart (page 58); cut four lengths. Size L = 25.5 cm (10 in.).
- Cotton bias binding, 4 cm (1½ in.) wide, to finish the neck and underarms/straps. See the Singlet block for the size charts (page 59). Size L = 2 × 24 cm (9½ in.) and 2 × 69 cm (27 in.).

TEMPLATE (SEE INSIDE COVER)

B3 Split facing

CUTTING PLAN, SIZE L

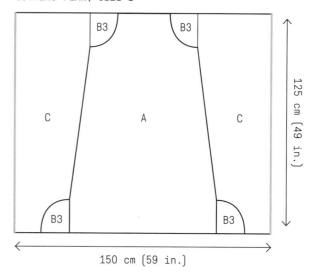

125 cm (49 in.)

150 cm (59 in.)

A Front body

B Side seam facing (template B3)

C Back body

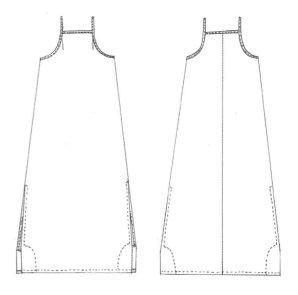

Cutting

STEP 1 Fold the fabric in half widthways, right sides together. Referring to the chart in the Singlet block, find the A/B and C/B widths for your size. Along the top edge of the fabric, measure the A/B distance from the fold and make a mark. Line up the B3 split facing template in the correct size with this mark and draw around the template. Repeat for the C/B width, this time measuring from the bottom left edge of the fabric. Mark one more straight line to join up the templates from bottom edge to bottom edge. This line becomes the side seam. Cut along the lines in order from 1 to 3.

STEP 2 Open out the front body piece (C). On the wrong side of the fabric, mark the darts on the top side neck edges using the measurements in the Single block (page 63).

Sewing

STEP 1 Following steps 1–3b of the Singlet block, sew the centre back seam on the back body (C) and the neck darts in the front body (A). Attach cotton tape to the underarms (see page 18). Attach bias binding to the neckline and underarms (see page 17), creating the shoulder straps in the process. After attaching the binding, overlock (serge) all four side seams separately. Prepare the side split facing pieces and attach them to the front and back, level with the hem, then press them back, away from the body. The fabric for this project already has the hem edges finished; if you are working with a fabric cut from the roll, attach the facing pieces in the same way as for the Singlet block, slightly up from the hem (page 65).

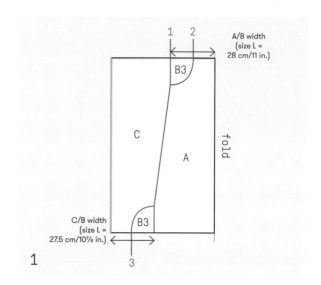

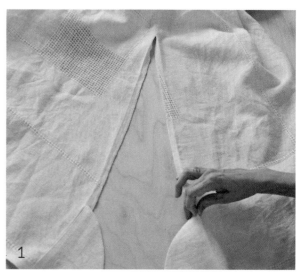

STEP 2   With right sides together, sew the side seams from the underarms downwards, stopping about 60 cm (24 in.) up from the hem edge; this unstitched section becomes the side split. At the underarms, topstitch over the binding on both sides of each side seam to hold the binding down neatly.

STEP 3   Press the seams open and press back and pin the unstitched sections of the side seams. Press the facings back, so that the garment and facings are wrong sides together, and pin in place (3a). Working from the wrong side of the garment and starting at the bottom edge of one facing, stitch up and around the curved edge of the facing through all layers, then pivot with the needle in the fabric and continue stitching along the turned-back section of the side seam. Continue until you reach the top of the split, then pivot again and stitch across the seam to the other side of the split and back down the other side, continuing all the way down and around the curved facing at the bottom (3b). Repeat at the other side split.

STEP 4   Hand stitch the bottom edge of the facings to the bottom edges of the hems. If you are using a fabric cut from the roll for this project, turn under and press a double 1-cm (⅜-in.) hem and stitch in place.

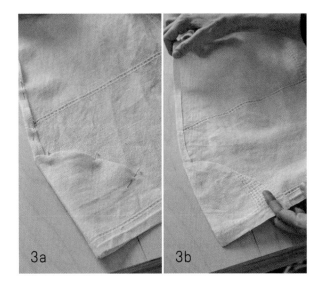

3a   3b

Tiered Skirt

SKILL LEVEL ●●○○○

BLOCK USED
Skirt (page 68)

TECHNIQUES USED
Elasticated waist casing
(page 20), Gathers
(page 21)

The tiered skirt has an additional gathered tier added to the bottom for extra fullness. The front and back top skirts are slightly shorter than the Skirt block. The length of this skirt is determined by the fabric width.

SIZING

This sample is a size S.

To size up or down, make the following adjustments:

- Add or remove 5 cm (2 in.) to the total length per size and adjust the A and B waist lengths to your chosen size by following the Skirt block measurements. The depth of all the tiers should be the same (for this size S cutting plan, all the tiers measure 31 cm/12 in.).
- The top skirt is slightly shorter than for the Skirt block (A/B width). For sizes XS–2XL, make the length 37 cm (15 in.). For sizes 3XL and above, make the length 40 cm (16½ in.). Keep in mind that adjusting the top skirt lengths will affect the depth of the tiers.

FABRIC USED

Cotton/linen, 185 gsm

Width: 130 cm (51 in.)

Length: 180 cm (79½ in.)

NOTIONS

- Elastic, 3 cm (1¼ in.) wide. Refer to the elastic size chart in the Skirt block on page 70 for the recommended length for your size. Size S = 65 cm (25½ in.).

CUTTING PLAN, SIZE S

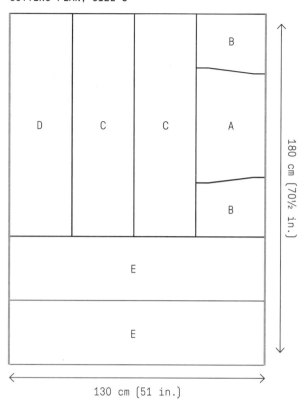

A   Front top skirt

B   Back top skirt

C   Front/back middle tier

D   Centre front bottom tier

E   Side/back bottom tier

Cutting

STEP 1   First, work out how much fabric you need. For sizes XS–2XL, deduct 37 cm (15 in.) from your total fabric width, then divide the remainder by 3: this gives you the depth of each tier of the skirt. For sizes 3XL and above, deduct 40 cm (16½ in.) from your fabric width and divide the remainder by 3. Find the fabric length for your size by referring to the chart on page 74 and add the depth of two tiers to this measurement; this gives you the total length of fabric that you need. For a size S, shown in the cutting plan below, the total fabric length required is 180 cm (70½ in.).

STEP 2   Cut your fabric to the required length. Across the bottom of the fabric, measure and mark out two horizontal strips, each one the depth of one tier. Cut along lines 1 and 2.

STEP 3   Fold the remaining fabric in half lengthways, right sides together. From the right-hand edge, measure and mark out pieces A and B, following step 2 of Cutting the Skirt block (page 75) and the diagram on the right for the A/B length. Divide the remaining fabric into three equal vertical strips. Cut along the lines in order from 3 to 6.

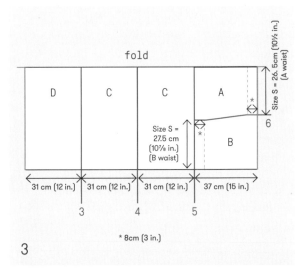

Sewing

STEP 1   Following steps 1–2 of the Skirt block (page 76), sew the centre back and side seams of the top skirt (A and B). Sew the waist casing and insert the elastic.

STEP 2   Place the front/back middle tiers (C) right sides together. Following steps 3a–3c of the Skirt block, sew the side seams. Gather the top edge, then attach the middle tier to the top tier.

STEP 3   With right sides together, sew the side/back bottom panels (E) together along one short edge; this is the centre back seam. Overlock the seam allowances together. Press the seam to one side.

STEP 4   With right sides together, sew the left and right short edges of the centre front bottom tier (D) to the left and right edges of the side/back bottom strip (E) to create a loop. Overlock (serge) the seam allowances together. Press the seams towards the back.

STEP 5   Gather the top edge of the bottom tier to fit the middle tier. With right sides together, match the centre back seam of the bottom tier to the centre back point of the middle tier, and the centre front point of the middle tier to the centre front point of the bottom tier. Sew the tiers together. Overlock the seam allowances together. Press the seam up.

          Note: On the bottom tier, the seams joining the side/back panel to the front panel will sit about one-quarter of the way into the front panel.

STEP 6   Turn up and press a double 1-cm (⅜-in.) hem. Pin and stitch in place.

Triangle Skirt

SKILL LEVEL ●●○○○

BLOCK USED
Skirt (page 68)

TECHNIQUES USED
In-seam pockets
(page 23), Elasticated
waist casing (page 20),
Binding (page 15)

The triangle skirt is a long A-line skirt that is a lengthened version of the triangular top sections of the Skirt block. It has high side splits, in-seam pockets and an attached waistband with inserted elastic.

SIZING

This sample is a size L.

Using this fabric width and pattern layout, sizes XS–XL will fit well into this width and length. For sizes above an XL, use a wider fabric or cut the pattern pieces going the other direction on your fabric, with skirt length determined by the fabric width.

To size up or down, make the following adjustments:

- Adjust the A and B waist lengths to your chosen size by following the Skirt block measurements (page 74).

FABRIC USED

Virgin wool/viscose blend, 185 gsm

Width: 145 cm (57 in.)

Length: 120 cm (47 in.)

NOTIONS

- Elastic, 5 cm (2 in.) wide. Refer to the Skirt block on page 70 to find the length you need for your size. Size L = 75 cm (29½ in.).
- Natural linen binding, 4 cm (1½ in.) wide, to finish one edge of the waistband. Determine the length by calculating your A waist + B waist x 2. Size L = 120 cm (47¼ in.).

CUTTING PLAN, SIZE L

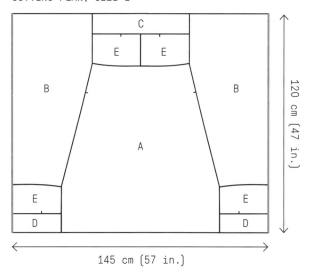

A   Front skirt

B   Back skirt

C   Front waistband

D   Back waistband

E   Pocket bag

Cutting

STEP 1 Fold the fabric in half widthways, right sides together. Referring to the Skirt block measurements (page 74), from the fold, measure and mark your A waist length along the top edge of the fabric. From the left-hand edge, measure and mark your B waist length along the bottom edge of the fabric.

STEP 2 Following the measurements in the diagram above, mark out the pieces. Then mark the notches on the front skirt (A) and pocket bags (E).

STEP 3 Cut along the lines in order from 1 to 6. Note that lines 3 and 5 curve slightly – refer to the diagram on the right. In line 6, you're cutting the pocket bags along the fold line.

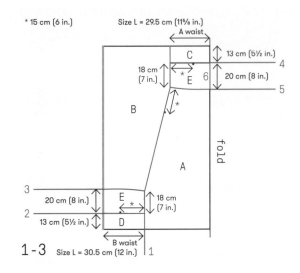

Sewing

STEP 1 Place the pocket bags (E) together in pairs, right sides together, and sew along the long, slightly curved edge and the short edge that measures 20 cm (8 in.). Overlock (serge) the seam allowances together.

STEP 2 With right sides together, matching the notches, place one layer of the notched edge of the pocket bag on the skirt side seam. Attach the pockets to the sides of the front skirt (A) – see In-seam pockets, page 23.

TIP The notch on the front skirt marks the bottom edge of the pocket opening (which measures 15 cm/6 in. in total) and should be matched to the notch on the pocket bag.

STEP 3 Place the back skirt pieces (B) right sides together and sew the centre back seam. Overlock the seam allowances together.

STEP 4 Overlock the side edges of the front and back skirts separately.

3 (Cutting)

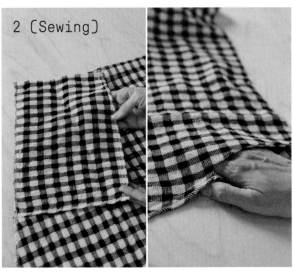

2 (Sewing)

STEP 5   Place the front and back skirts right sides together and sew the side seams, working downwards from the top and finishing about 30 cm (12 in.) up from the hem edge. Press the seams open and press the unstitched section to the wrong side in line with the seam allowances.

STEP 6   Working from the wrong side, stitch along the splits to hold down the pressed-under seam allowances. Start at one hem edge and continue up to the start of the split, turn and stitch across, then continue the stitching down the other side to the hem. Turn under and press a double 1-cm (⅜-in.) hem and stitch in place.

STEP 7   With right sides together, place the back waistbands (D) on top of the front waistband (C) and sew together along the short edges. Press the seams open.

STEP 8   Apply binding (see page 17) to one long edge of the waistband. Cut off any excess binding after sewing.

STEP 9   With right sides together, sew the centre back seam of the waistband. Press the seam open.

STEP 10   With right sides together, matching the side and centre back seams, sew the unfinished edge of the waistband to the top of the skirt. Press the seam and waistband up.

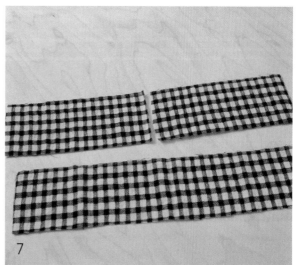

STEP 11   Press the waistband in half widthways, wrong sides together. Working from the right side of the garment, stitch 'in the ditch' (on top of the previous seam line), making sure you catch the bottom bound edge of the waistband in the stitching on the inside of the skirt, leaving a 5-cm (2-in.) opening at the centre back.

STEP 12   Insert the elastic (see page 20). Stitch the opening at the centre back closed.

STEP 13   Stretch the elastic out evenly and pin it in place at the side and centre back seams. Stitch over the waistband at the side and centre back seams, stitching a vertical stitch line through all layers to hold the elastic in place.

Gathered Shirt Dress

SKILL LEVEL ●●●○○

BLOCKS USED
Shirt (page 78) and
Skirt (page 69)

TECHNIQUES USED
Binding (page 15),
Inserting a sleeve
(page 19), Gathers
(page 21), Sewing and
attaching a collar and
button placket (page 25),
Buttons and buttonholes
(page 29)

This dress uses a shortened version of the Shirt block with gathered panels from the Skirt block. This dress is made using two different vintage fabrics, so the pattern layout is broken up into two sections, but you could join them together and use the same fabric for all if you wish.

SIZING

The shirt section is suitable for sizes S–XL and the skirt is a free size due to the gathers.

This is a great style for split sizing – for example, if you are smaller on the top with curvy hips.

To size up or down, use a wider or narrower fabric width.

FABRIC USED

Vintage cotton tablecloth and sheet. Offcuts have been saved for patchworking into the Quilted Jacket project on page 182.

This project uses two different fabrics – the individual measurements used for the shirt and skirt are shown below.

- Shirt: Width 135 cm (53 in.); Length 70 cm (27½ in.)
- Skirt: Width 135 cm (53 in.); Length 150 cm (59 in.)

NOTIONS

- Cotton bias binding, 4 cm (1½ in.) wide, to finish the collar. See the Shirt block on page 80 for more information.
  You will need 2 × 20 cm (8 in.).
- Corozo nut buttons, 1.5 cm (⅝ in.) in diameter.
  You will need 3 buttons for the centre front placket.

TEMPLATES (SEE INSIDE COVER)

B5 Back neck facing

E Sleeve head curve

CUTTING PLAN

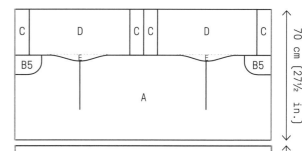

70 cm (27½ in.)

150 cm (59 in.)

This cutting plan has been broken up into two sections, as a different fabric has been used for the shirt and skirt.

135 cm (53 in.)

A Front/back body

B Back neck facing (template B5)

C Collar

D Sleeves

E Sleeve head curve (template E)

F Front/back skirt

Cutting

STEP 1   Fold both fabrics in half widthways, right sides together.

STEP 2   Mark out the pieces for the shirt, following steps 2 and 3 of Cutting the shirt block (page 84). For the skirt section, simply fold the fabric in half lengthways and draw a horizontal line across the fabric.

STEP 3   Cut along the lines in order from 1 to 7.

STEP 4   Referring to the diagram in step 5 of the Shirt block (page 85), cut notches in the front and back bodies (A) and the centre point of the shoulders on the sleeve pieces (D).

Sewing

STEP 1   Sew the shirt section, following steps 1a–4b of the Shirt block (pages 86–87).

STEP 2   Overlap the button plackets, right side over left side, by 3 cm (1¼ in.) at the bottom and sew though all layers to hold the plackets in place.

STEP 3   Turn under the ends of the sleeves by 1 cm (⅜ in.) and press, then turn up the sleeve hem to your chosen length and press again. Topstitch in place.

STEP 4   Work three horizontal buttonholes (see page 29) on the right placket, positioning the first one 1.5 cm (⅝ in.) from the top and the third one about 6 cm (2½ in.) up from the hem, with the second buttonhole centred in between. Sew the three buttons to the left placket to correspond.

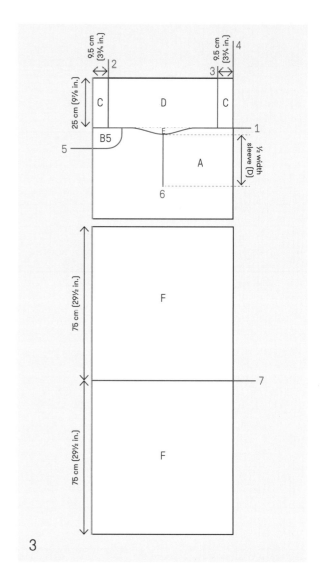

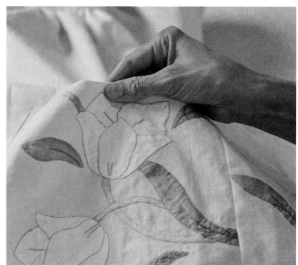

STEP 5 Place the skirt panels right sides together and sew the side seams. Overlock (serge) the seam allowances together and press the seams towards the back.

STEP 6 Gather (see page 21) the top edge of the skirt to fit the bottom edge of the shirt.

STEP 7 With right sides together, sew the skirt to the shirt (7a). Overlock the seam allowances together and press the seam up (7b).

STEP 8 This project uses the pre-bound edge of the vintage fabric as the finished hem of the skirt (shown in the image). If you are using a fabric cut from the roll, turn under and press a double 1-cm (⅜-in.) hem around the bottom edge of the skirt and stitch in place.

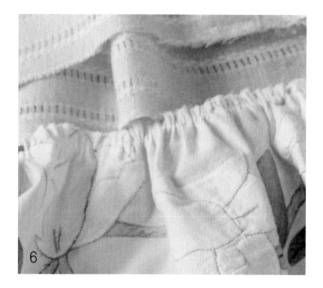

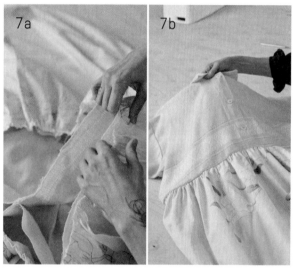

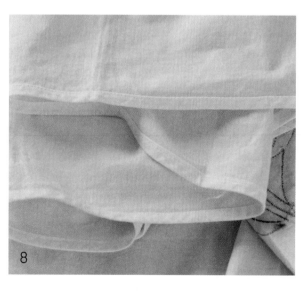

Shirt Dress

BLOCK USED
Shirt (page 78)

TECHNIQUES USED
Binding (page 15),
Inserting a sleeve
(page 19), Sewing and
attaching a collar and
button placket (page 25),
Buttons and buttonholes
(page 29)

The shirt dress is a lengthened version of the Shirt block. The buttonholes run vertically instead of horizontally and there is topstitch detailing around the collar.

SIZING

This sample is a one size, suitable for sizes XS–2XL.

To size up, you can rotate the pattern pieces to go in the other direction (with the hem running along the selvedge edge) and add extra to the width. Keep in mind that if you rotate the pattern pieces your fabric width will determine the finished length of the garment.

FABRIC USED

Organic cotton, 106 gsm

Width: 154 cm (60½ in.)

Length: 130 cm (51 in.)

NOTIONS

• Cotton binding, 4 cm (1½ in.) wide, to finish the collar. See the Shirt block on page 80 for more information. You will need two 20-cm (8-in.) lengths.

• Corozo nut buttons, 1.5 cm (⅝ in.) in diameter. You will need 7 buttons for the centre front placket.

TEMPLATES (SEE INSIDE COVER)

B5 Back neck facing

E Sleeve head curve

CUTTING PLAN

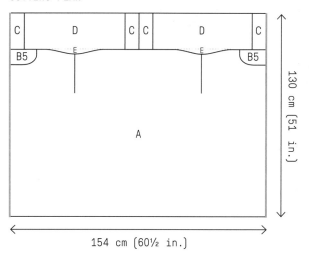

154 cm (60½ in.)

130 cm (51 in.)

A Front/back body

B Back neck facing (template B5)

C Collar

D Sleeve

E Sleeve head curve (template E)

Cutting

STEP 1   Fold the fabric in half widthways, right sides together.

STEP 2   Mark out the pieces, following steps 2 and 3 of Cutting the shirt block (page 84).

STEP 3   Cut along the lines in order from 1 to 6.

STEP 4   Referring to the diagram in step 5 of the Shirt block (page 85), cut notches in the front and back bodies (A) and at the centre point of the shoulders on the sleeve pieces (D).

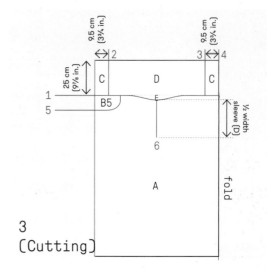

3
[Cutting]

Sewing

STEP 1   Following steps 1a–3a of the Shirt block (pages 86–87), sew the shirt dress up to the point at which you are ready to attach the collar.

STEP 2   Using matching thread, edge stitch around the long folded edge and the two short sides of the collar, leaving the open edge unstitched.

STEP 3   Attach the collar to the neck of the shirt and complete the shirt dress following steps 3b–5b (pages 87–88) of the Shirt block, working the buttonholes vertically, not horizontally. Position the centre of the first buttonhole approximately 2 cm (¾ in.) from the top and space the other six evenly, about 11.5 cm (4½ in.) apart (3a) Sew on buttons to correspond (3b).

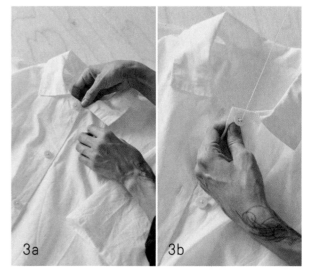

3a

3b

Vintage Shirt

SKILL LEVEL ●●●○○

BLOCK USED
Shirt (page 78)

TECHNIQUES USED
Binding (page 15),
Inserting a sleeve
(page 19), Elasticated
waist casing (page 20),
Sewing and attaching a
collar and button placket
(page 25), Patch pockets
(page 22), Buttons and
buttonholes (page 29)

This shirt has long sleeves with elastic inserted inside the sleeve hems to gather them in at the wrist. There is also a small patch pocket on the front. It is made using a vintage embroidered sheet with lace detailing. The fabric used is very narrow, so to get slightly more width in the body a contrasting white fabric has been added to centre front body edges as a facing for the underside of the button plackets. This shirt has a wider collar than the one in the Shirt block and the collar has no centre back seam.

SIZING

The sample and pattern layout are a one-size pattern, suitable for sizes S–M.

To size up, use a wider fabric. Refer to the Shirt block measurement charts (page 81) for details of what fabric widths are suitable for what body measurements. If you are using a narrow fabric for a larger size, you can extend the width of the piece by referring to the alternative cutting plan shown in the Shirt block (page 89).

FABRIC USED

Vintage cotton embroidered sheet

Width: 116 cm (45½ in.)

Length: 130 cm (51 in.)

NOTIONS

• White light- to medium-weight cotton for the centre front facing pieces (G). You will need two pieces 5.5 cm (2⅛ in.) wide x 51 cm (20 in.) long.

• Medium-weight iron-on interfacing for the centre front facing pieces (G). You will need two pieces 5.5 cm (2⅛ in.) wide x 51 cm (20 in.) long.

• Cotton binding, 4 cm (1½ in.) wide, to finish the collar. See the Shirt block on page 80 for more information. You will need two pieces 20 cm (8 in.) long.

• Corozo nut buttons, 1.5 cm (⅝ in.) in diameter. You will need five buttons for the centre front placket.

• Elastic, 1 cm (⅜ in.) wide, to insert into the sleeve hems. You will need two pieces 25 cm (10 in.) long.

TEMPLATES (SEE INSIDE COVER)

B5 Back neck facing – remove 3.5 cm (1 ⅜ in.) from the centre front

E Sleeve head curve

CUTTING PLAN, SIZE S–M

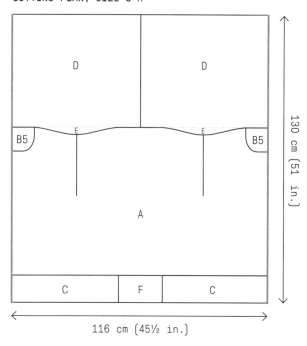

130 cm (51 in.)

116 cm (45½ in.)

A Front/back body

B Back neck facing – remove 3.5 cm (1⅜ in.) from the centre front edge (B5 template)

C Collar

D Sleeves

E Sleeve head curve (template E)

F Breast pocket

G Centre front facing

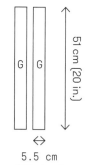

51 cm (20 in.)

5.5 cm (2⅛ in.)

Cutting

STEP 1   Fold the fabric in half widthways, right sides together.

STEP 2   Mark out the pieces, using the measurements in the diagram on the right and following steps 2 and 3 of Cutting the shirt block (page 84), making sure you remove 3.5 cm (1⅜ in.) from the centre front edge of template B5 first.

STEP 3   Cut along the lines in order from 1 to 6.

STEP 4   Mark and cut notches 5.5 cm (2⅛ in.) and 5 cm (2 in.) from the centre back.

STEP 5   Cut two pieces of contrasting fabric and two pieces of iron-on interfacing for the centre front facings (G). The length of the facings should be the same as the centre front body length, as shown in the diagram.

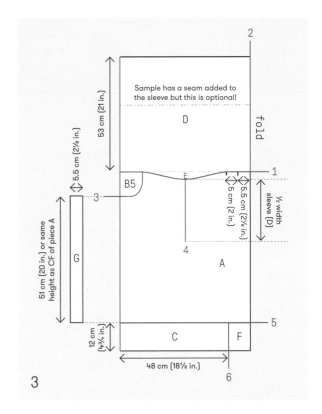

Sewing

STEP 1   Following steps 1–3a of the Shirt block (pages 86–87), sew the centre back pleat, insert the sleeves and sew and attach the collar. Note that the collar on this shirt does not have a centre back seam. In step 3a, when you attach the binding to the neck, attach it all the way to the centre front edges.

STEP 2   Apply interfacing to the wrong side of the centre front facings (G). With right sides together, sew the facings to the centre front edges. Press the facings and seam allowances away from the body and understitch on the facing side to hold down the seam allowance.

STEP 3   Following step 3b of the Shirt block (page 87), attach the back neck facing.

STEP 4   Follow step 4b of the Shirt block (page 87) to create the centre front button plackets. The steps here are exactly the same, except that the seam that joins the centre front facings to the bodies should be treated as the second 'notch' point to which you fold back the centre front edges. The raw edges of the facings should be turned under by 1 cm (⅜ in.) and pressed.

STEP 5   Turn under the ends of the sleeves by 1 cm (⅜ in.) and press, then turn up the sleeve hem by 1.5 cm (⅝ in.) and press again. Topstitch in place, leaving an opening of 5 cm (2 in.) near the underarm seam to create a casing for the elastic.

STEP 6   Thread the elastic through the casing (6a – see page 20), then topstitch the opening closed (6b).

STEP 7   Turn up and press a double 1-cm (⅜-in.) hem around the bottom of the shirt and topstitch in place.

STEP 8   Turn the top edge of the pocket to the wrong side by 1 cm (⅜ in.) and press, then turn under 7 cm (2¾ in.) and press again. Topstitch in place. Press the side and bottom edges of the pocket to the wrong side by 1 cm (⅜ in.) and sew the pocket to one side of the front, about 25 cm (10 in.) down from the shoulder (see Patch pockets, page 22).

STEP 9   Work five horizontal buttonholes (see page 29) down the right placket, positioning the first one 1.5 cm (⅝ in.) from the top and the other four approximately 9.5 cm (3¾ in.) apart. Sew the five buttons to the left placket to correspond.

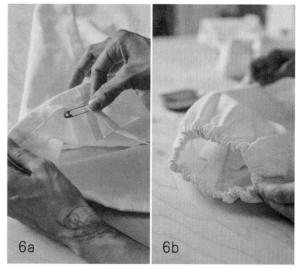

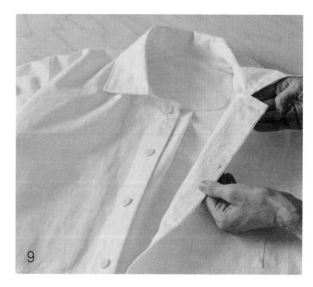

Quilted Jacket

SKILL LEVEL ●●●●○

BLOCK USED
Shirt (page 78)

TECHNIQUES USED
Binding (page 15),
Inserting a sleeve
(page 19), Patch pockets
(page 22)

The quilted jacket is patchworked together using cotton offcuts from the blocks and vintage fabric offcuts from some of the projects. It is made up of three layers of fabric: a patchworked outer layer, a middle layer of wadding (batting), and a lining, all quilted together before being cut out and sewn. The pattern layout is very similar to the Shirt block, except that the collar pieces and back neck facings are used as pockets. All edges of the garment are finished with a contrasting binding.

SIZING

This sample is a one size, suitable for sizes XS–2XL.

To size up or down, you can use a wider or narrower fabric to add or remove width from the body.

FABRIC USED

Outer layer: Re-purposed cotton offcuts taken from the blocks and vintage fabrics left over from the Gathered Shirt Dress, patchworked to a width of 160 cm (63 in.) to fit to the width of the lining

Wadding: Poly/cotton wadding (batting)

Lining: Cotton gauze, 140 gsm, 160 cm (63 in.) wide

Finished size of the quilted fabric with all three layers:

Width: 160 cm (63 in.)

Length: 100 cm (39½ in.)

NOTIONS

• Linen binding, 4 cm (1½ in.) wide, to finish the shoulder seams, armhole and underarm seams, neck, hems and pocket edges. You will need around 7 m (7½ yd).

TEMPLATES (SEE INSIDE COVER)

B5 Breast pocket – remove 2.5 cm (1 in.) from the centre front

E Sleeve head curve

CUTTING PLAN

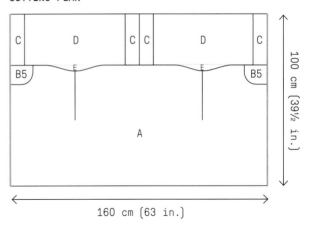

100 cm (39½ in.)

160 cm (63 in.)

A   Front/back body

B   Breast pocket (template B5)

C   Hip pockets

D   Sleeves

E   Sleeve head curve (template E)

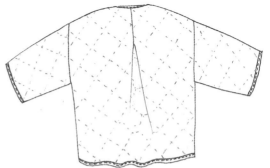

Patchworking

For this project, you have to patchwork pieces of scrap fabric together and quilt it before marking out and cutting the garment pieces.

STEP 1   Sew pieces of scrap fabric together using different-sized squares and rectangles until you have a piece the size you need. You may find it easier to make several smaller sections and then sew them all together to make one large piece at the end.

STEP 2   Press all the seams open.

TIP   It's a good idea to make your finished fabric slightly larger than the required width and length of the project – around 2.5 cm (1 in.) added to the length and width should be enough. This is because when you quilt all your layers together at the end, the fabric will shrink to become slightly smaller in size.

Quilting

STEP 1   Cut the wadding (batting) and lining to the same size as the patchwork. Place all layers together, with the right sides of the fabrics facing outwards and the wadding in the middle. Pin to hold everything together.

STEP 2   Using tailor's chalk or a dissolvable fabric marker pen, mark evenly spaced diagonal lines 10 cm (4 in.) apart to create diamond shapes (2a and 2b). Place pins along the lines, around 15 cm (6 in.) apart, to hold all three layers together (2c).

STEP 3   Sew down all diagonal lines one at a time, going through all layers of the fabric and removing the pins as you go.

STEP 4   Press the fabric and measure to make sure it is the right size. Trim all three layers level.

2a (Quilting)

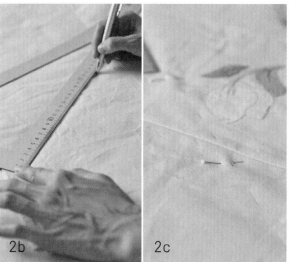

2b   2c

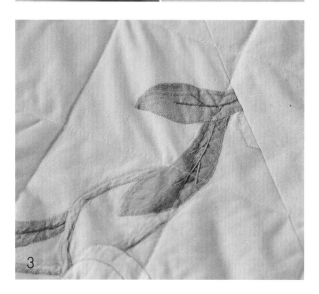

3

Cutting

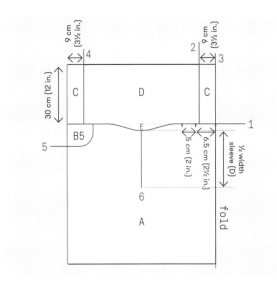

STEP 1 Fold the quilted fabric in half widthways, right sides together.

STEP 2 Before starting, make sure you have removed 2.5 cm (1 in.) from the centre front edge of template B5. Mark out the pieces, using the measurements in the diagram on the right and following steps 2 and 3 of Cutting the shirt block (page 84).

STEP 3 Cut along the lines in order from 1 to 6.

STEP 4 Mark and cut notches 6.5 cm (2½ in.) from the centre back and 5 cm (2 in.) from the first notch. The notches 6.5 cm (2½ in.) from the centre back are for the pleat; the ones 5 cm (2 in.) from the first notch are for the back neck/where the front neck finishes.

Sewing

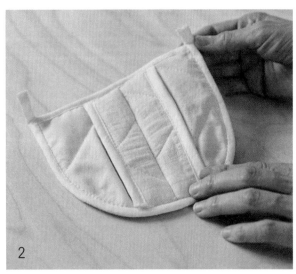

STEP 1 Bind (see page 17) the short straight side of each of the two breast pocket pieces (B). With right sides together, taking a 2.5-cm (1-in.) seam allowance, sew the pocket pieces together along this edge and press the seam open.

STEP 2 Bind the top edge of the breast pocket and then the curved edges, leaving a little excess binding at each end to tuck under at the top.

STEP 3 Bind one long edge of each hip pocket piece (C). Place the hip pockets right sides together in pairs and sew together along this edge, taking a 1-cm (⅜-in.) seam allowance. Press the seams open. Bind the top edge of each pocket and then press 10 cm (4 in.) to the wrong side. Topstitch down the sides to hold down the folded section of the pocket. Bind the bottom edge and then the sides, leaving a little excess binding top and bottom to tuck under.

STEP 4 Pin the pockets in place, tucking in the excess binding where necessary to neaten the corners. Position the breast pocket around 28 cm (11 in.) down from the shoulder and 9 cm (3½ in.) in from the centre front on the outer layer (4a) and the hip pockets around 42 cm (16½ in.) down from the shoulder and 8 cm (3 in.) in from the centre front on the lining (4b).

STEP 5 Topstitch the pockets in place; your stitching will be visible from both sides.

STEP 6 Sew the centre back pleat of the jacket (see Shirt block, Sewing, step 1 on page 86). Hand stitch across the pleat about 12 cm (4¾ in.) from the top through all layers to hold it in place.

STEP 7 Bind the edges in this order: the curved front necklines, the hem, and the centre front edges (7a and 7b), turning the binding in neatly at the top and bottom of the centre front.

STEP 8 Following step 2a of the Shirt block (page 86), with right sides together, sew the shoulder seams, making sure the edge of the front neckline matches the back notches. Bind the seam allowances together, continuing across the back neckline.

STEP 9 Bind the underarm edges of the sleeves separately. With right sides together, following steps 2b–2c of the Shirt block (page 86), sew the underarm seams. Press the seam allowances open. Insert the sleeves into the armholes and stitch in place (see page 19). Bind the seams together.

STEP 10 Bind the sleeve hem, turning in one end of the binding at the start and overlapping the other end of the binding over this section by around 1.5 cm (½ in.) to create a neat join.

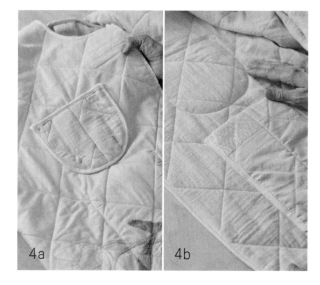

4a   4b

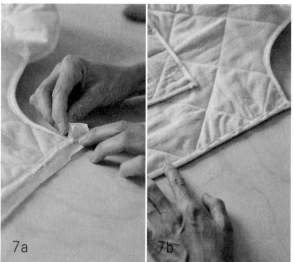

7a   7b

8

Index

Suppliers

My thanks to the following companies for tools and fabrics used in the book:

Tools and equipment

- **Husqvarna** (www.husqvarnaviking.com) for the sewing machine (Husqvarna Viking Opal 690Q) and overlocker/serger (Husqvarna Viking AMBER Air S 400).
- **Toolly** (www.toolly.de) and Beyond Measure (www.shopbeyondmeasure.co.uk) for general sewing equipment.
- **Siebenblau** (www.siebenblau.de) for organic cotton sewing and overlocking thread.

Fabrics

- **Beyond Measure** (www.shopbeyondmeasure.co.uk) for the organic cotton bias binding used in several of the projects.
- **Lebenskleidung** (www.lebenskleidung.com) for the organic cotton ribbing used in the Sweater and the organic popeline used in the Shirt Dress and Vintage Shirt.
- **Merchant and Mills** (www.merchantandmills.com) for the heavyweight cotton jacquard used in the Sweater, the washed linen used in the Wrap Top and Shorts, and the cotton twill used in the Boiler Suit.
- **Self Made** (www.selfmade.com) for the checked linen used in the Tiered Skirt.
- **Siebenblau** (www.siebenblau.de) for the natural linen bias strips used in the Playsuit.

Further Resources

Here are some excellent additional resources if you want to learn more about the history of ZWPC:

- *Cut my Cote*, Dorothy K. Burnham (Royal Ontario Museum, 1990)
- *Clothing from the Hands That Weave*, Anita Luvera Mayer (Echo Point Books & Media, 2016)
- *Zero Waste Fashion Design*, Timo Rissanen and Holly McQuillan (Bloomsbury Visual Arts, 2018)

Acknowledgements

Thank you to the most amazing team at Quadrille who worked on this book with me: editors Oreolu Grillo and Harriet Butt, for being so open to my ideas and helping bring them to life, designer Emily Lapworth for putting together an amazing layout and being so patient with me throughout all the cover changes, photographer Emli Bendixen – we had a lot to get through in a short time, but your talent and natural eye for capturing the making process and the garments made it a breeze – and project editor Sarah Hoggett for working so hard on this and being so incredibly thorough and precise with the text.

I'd like to thank my dad Karl-Gustav and uncle Lars for kindly allowing us to use the family farm as a location and for being so generous and helpful with their time. My late grandmother who lived here was a source of inspiration to me as a child and into adulthood with the textiles she made, with her weaving, embroidery, up-cycling, and repair, no bells and whistles, always simple, practical, and useful. To my partner Sam Grose: we live together, work together and do everything together basically, but somehow we still aren't sick of each other! You have been so supportive throughout all of this, with the late nights and extra hours I needed to do, taking the reins with the kids and generally keeping everything together! My eldest daughter Astrid, for always having such great advice and opinions – especially when it comes to fashion and style! My youngest daughter Aila, for providing plenty of cuddles when I needed them. Thanks to my mum Katharine and sister Anna, for having long chats with me about the book and my ideas. And to my friends Edith, Nastassia and Lauren, for always being there for me to bounce things off of and offer honest and constructive advice and feedback when I needed it!

And to someone who has been in my thoughts every single day, who was always the most vibrant and well dressed in the room. I am forever grateful for the time we got to spend together, growing up and becoming 'adults' in Melbourne. Your passionate, wild and magical spirit will always inspire me. This book is dedicated to you, Scarlet.

MANAGING DIRECTOR
Sarah Lavelle

SENIOR COMMISSIONING EDITOR
Harriet Butt

PROJECT EDITOR
Sarah Hoggett

ASSISTANT EDITOR
Oreolu Grillo

ART DIRECTOR & DESIGNER
Emily Lapworth

PHOTOGRAPHER
Emli Bendixen

STYLIST
Charlotte Melling

HAIR & MAKE-UP
Sherin at Ksting

MODELS
**Birgitta, Jazmine,
Nastassia, Sarah, Shoko**

HEAD OF PRODUCTION
Stephen Lang

PRODUCTION CONTROLLER
Martina Georgieva

Published in 2023 by Quadrille Publishing Limited

Quadrille
52–54 Southwark Street
London SE1 1UN
quadrille.com

Text © Birgitta Helmersson 2023
Photography © Emli Bendixen 2023
Design © Quadrille 2023

ISBN 978 178 713 924 4

Reprinted in 2023 (three times), 2024 (twice)
10 9 8 7 6

Printed in China using vegetable-based inks

MIX
Paper | Supporting
responsible forestry
FSC® C018179